43RD DIVISION INVESTITURE

LIEUT.-COLONEL W. ROBERTS, 4TH DORSETS, RECEIVES THE D.S.O. 5.12.44

FROM NORMANDY TO THE WESER

*The War History of the
Fourth Battalion the Dorset Regiment
June, 1944—May, 1945*

The Naval & Military Press Ltd

Published by
The Naval & Military Press Ltd
5 Riverside, Brambleside, Bellbrook
Industrial Estate, Uckfield, East Sussex,
TN22 1QQ England

Tel: +44 (0) 1825 749494
Fax: +44 (0) 1825 765701

www.naval-military-press.com
www.nmarchive.com

In reprinting in facsimile from the original, any imperfections are inevitably reproduced and the quality may fall short of modern type and cartographic standards.

FOREWORD

THIS is the gallant story of the original Territorial Battalion of the Dorset Regiment, their training in England and their fighting in North-West Europe.

The accounts of some of the Episodes written by the Officers who actually took part in them should appeal to All Ranks who served in this Battalion, and the Relatives and Friends of those who are on the Roll of Honour.

The spirit which shines through all the battles and engagements was created by the Volunteers who gave up their spare time in the days of peace.

> D. BAXTER, Lieut.-Col.,
> Honorary Colonel.

AUTHOR'S NOTE

ALTHOUGH commissioned in the 4th Dorsets very shortly before the outbreak of war, the writer of this brief history never had the honour to serve with that or any other unit of the Regiment, nor did he take part in the North-West European or any other campaign. He has, therefore, no knowledge whatever of regimental soldiering or of active service conditions, and has been obliged to rely, in the writing of this history, entirely on official and unofficial written documents, and on the personal reminiscences of others, a debt which he has been very careful to acknowledge in the footnotes.

When it was necessary to refer to the overall strategic situation, General of the Army Dwight D. Eisenhower's 'Complete Report by the Supreme Commander on the War in Europe from the Day of Invasion to the Day of Victory' (referred to in the footnotes as 'Eisenhower') has been used. The Battalion's War Diary (referred to in the footnotes as 'W.D.' only when it seemed necessary to differentiate between it and some less official source) provided the bare bones of the story: for detail, the writer has used 'The Story of the 5th Battalion The Dorsetshire Regiment in North-West Europe' by Majors G. R. Hartwell, G. R. Pack and M. A. Edwards ('Hartwell'), Lieut.-Colonel J. L. Wood's 'Notes, 12th July to 6th August' ('Wood'), Lieut.-Colonel H. E. Cowie's 'Brief Outline of Events from their Landing in Normandy until 12th July 1944' ('Cowie'), Lieut.-Colonel W. Q. Roberts' 'Report on the Activities of the 4th Battalion The Dorsetshire Regiment' ('Roberts'), and an unidentified 'Report on the 4th Dorsets' Doings from July 13th to September 26th' ('Unidentified Report'). Particular mention should also be made of the exhaustive diary kept throughout the campaign by Sergt. (eventually Captain) W. Caines ('Caines'). This account cannot be regarded as in any way official, but it has been invaluable as a source of local colour and its author has a remarkable knack of making his narrative live. It has been quoted from largely.

The writer wishes to thank Lieut.-Colonel G. L. Symonds for reading and criticising the original draft and suggesting many improvements, and for writing accounts of the battles at Eterville and in the Reichswald: Lieut.-Colonel W. Q. Roberts for writing accounts of the occupation of 'Dorset Wood', the battle in the Reichswald and the capture of Millingen: Major M. Whittle for writing accounts of the battle at Maltot and of Arnhem: Major G. Matthews for writing accounts of the occupation of 'Dorset Wood' and of the Battalion's tour of duty in Italy; and Captain S. Elvery for making copies of the citations. He wishes to express particular gratitude to Lieut.-Colonel J. F. F. Lathbury, R.E., of the Survey Branch, H.Q., B.A.O.R., for the infinite trouble he took in providing the 1-inch and ¼-inch maps without which the history could never have been written, and which it proved impossible to obtain through the normal channels in England.

G.J.B.W.

CONTENTS

		PAGE
I	ENGLAND	1
II	NORMANDY	5
III	THE BREAK-THROUGH AND THE PURSUIT ...	18
IV	ARNHEM ...	29
V	ON THE DEFENSIVE ...	39
VI	THE INVASION OF GERMANY	50
VII	THE COLLAPSE	65
VIII	ARMY OF OCCUPATION	75
	HONOURS AND AWARDS	81
	CITATIONS ...	83

LIST OF ILLUSTRATIONS

FACING PAGE

43RD DIVISION INVESTITURE. LIEUT.-COLONEL W. Q. ROBERTS, 4TH DORSETS, RECEIVES THE D.S.O. 5.12.44 ... ... *Frontispiece*

MR. MACKENZIE KING INTRODUCES GENERAL SMUTS TO CANADIAN OFFICERS SERVING WITH THE 4TH BATTALION THE DORSET REGIMENT. 12.5.44 16

THE CARRIER PLATOON OF THE 4TH BATTALION THE DORSET REGIMENT CROSSING THE PONTOON BRIDGE ACROSS THE SEINE. PICTURE TAKEN FROM VERNONNET. 27.8.44 17

43RD DIVISION INVESTITURE. SERGT. F. STRETCH, 4TH BATTALION THE DORSET REGIMENT, AWARDED THE M.M. 24.5.45... ... 80

PTE. H. APPS, 4TH BATTALION THE DORSET REGIMENT, AWARDED THE M.M. 24.5.45 81

MAPS

		PAGE
1	CHEUX, ETERVILLE AND MALTOT ...	10
2	CAUMONT, ONDEFONTAINE AND MONT PINCON	21
3	FRESNES ...	25
4	ARNHEM	32
5	THE SITTARD TRIANGLE	43
6	THE REICHSWALD	54
7	THE CROSSING OF THE RHINE AND MILLINGEN ...	62

I

ENGLAND

GERMANY launched her unprovoked and unheralded attack on Poland during the early hours of Friday, September 1st, 1939, and on the same day His Majesty the King signed the order for the embodiment of the Territorial Army. All that day and the next officers and men arrived at Dorchester in response to telegrams, and late on the afternoon of September 2nd the 4th Dorsets moved to Weymouth.

The War Office in its wisdom decided to move territorial units away from their peace-time areas, so that training might not be hampered by the attractions of home life, regardless of the fact that it could give them little or no equipment with which to train. The concentration area allotted to 130 Infantry Brigade, of which the Battalion was part, was on the borders of Wiltshire and Somerset, and the Headquarters and the other two battalions of the Brigade were installed at Frome well before Christmas. The 4th, however, did not move to Cucklington, in Somerset, until March 3rd, 1940, so that, but for a few weeks in the Verne Citadel, Portland, in September and October, 1939, it was to stay at Weymouth for exactly six months.

Its mode of life during this period was the most depressing that the High Command could devise for men who were aching for action at a time of national stress: the Battalion had, indeed, a few operational commitments in the nature of guarding vulnerable points and, should it be necessary, aid to the civil population, but in the absence of nearly all equipment its primary function of training for action in the field could not properly be fulfilled, and the Winter proved to be largely one of route marches and lectures by day, and cold nights spent on hard floors with insufficient blankets.

The end of this frustrating Winter, which both officers and men bore with philosophic fortitude, came in May, 1940. The Germans attacked in the West on May 10th, and when, on the evening of the 12th, they penetrated the defences along the Franco-Belgian frontier, and it became obvious that neither French, Belgian, Dutch or British armies could stop them, it was clear that, for the first time in nearly a century and a half, England was no longer safe from invasion from abroad. The half trained, half equipped Territorial force at home became almost overnight the bulk of a field force that might have to go into action at any moment, stiffened only by the veterans who had brought the wisdom of their hard earned experience back from Dunkirk, but who had been obliged to leave all their equipment behind them. An upper structure of Armies and Corps was hastily formed, and late in May the 43rd Infantry Division, of which the 130th Brigade formed a part, moved to Hertfordshire under command of 4th Corps, which formed the G.H.Q. mobile reserve North of the Thames, charged with the defence of North London and with the eventual role of moving to defend the coast of East Anglia anywhere between the Wash and Southend.

The 4th Dorsets moved to Berkhamsted on the 23rd May, and immediately settled down to a life that, in its essentials, was to last for almost exactly four years. There were road blocks and machine-gun posts to be sited, constructed and manned during the hours of darkness: occasionally there were crashed enemy aircraft to be guarded and enemy airmen to be captured; patrols had to be organised to investigate reported cases of light signals and parachute landings, an operational commitment that decreased as the national spy-fever abated. Above all, training continued, becoming more and more intensive as equipment was supplied, and as the next four years passed and the danger of invasion lessened, the Battalion was increasingly absent from its location taking part in divisional, corps or army exercises.

On September 8th, during a corps exercise, the code word 'Cromwell' was received, the signal that invasion was imminent, and the whole Brigade immediately moved to its operational concentration area in Hatfield Forest, near Bishop's Stortford. The High Command, probably wisely, had diligently put it about that an invasion was to be desired as offering the best chance of beating the Germans quickly; as this propaganda had been widely believed, there was naturally widespread disappointment when, on September 22nd, the 'Stand Down' order was received.

The Battalion next spent a month at Hertford, and then moved to 'Hellfire Corner', the most nearly operational part of England, taking up its station in Dover Castle on the 9th November. While there it shared the responsibility for the defence of Dover against attack by land or sea and worked at improving the existing defences of the area. It came in for its fair share of enemy shelling and bombing and was able for the first time to make its presence felt by the enemy when, on the 14th, one of its light machine-guns shot down a German aircraft.

At Dover the Battalion had been in sight of the enemy, at least in clear weather, and one officer made a habit of going every morning to the Naval gun room to see if a British bomb had yet demolished his own house on the cliffs of Calais. But even this remote contact came to an end in February, 1941, when the Battalion moved to Canterbury, after which it was destined not to see the French coast again until it landed in Normandy in June, 1944.

Six weeks at Canterbury were succeeded by six weeks at Sturry, nine months at Herne Bay, and a year and three months at Sandwich, where the change was made from defensive to offensive training. In May, 1943, it moved to Waldershare Park, near Dover, and exactly a month later to Cliftonville, where it remained for four months until, on the 4th August, 1943, it moved to Bexhill-on-Sea, its last station in England, from which it was to move ten months later to Normandy.

Early in 1944 action was at last in sight. On February 4th the Battalion marched to Hastings, where the whole of the 130th Brigade was inspected by General Sir Bernard Montgomery, Commander-in-Chief of 21st Army Group; on the 12th May it was visited by the Prime Minister, the Rt. Hon. Winston Spencer

Churchill, the Dominions Prime Ministers and Field-Marshal Sir Alan Brooke, Chief of the Imperial General Staff, who watched a demonstration by its Pioneer Platoon. The War Diary records that the week-end of the 27th May was occupied by intensive preparations for movement overseas, and Lieut.-Colonel H. E. Cowie, the Commanding Officer, attended a conference of unit commanders held by General Montgomery.

On June 6th, 'D-Day', the British and American Armies made their first landings on the coast of Normandy, and the Battalion was ordered to be ready to move at twelve hours' notice. On the 7th, the General Officer Commanding 43rd Division held a conference for all officers and warrant officers at which he explained the progress and intentions of the Allied Expeditionary Force; on the 10th copies of the letter from General Dwight D. Eisenhower, Supreme Commander of the Allied Expeditionary Force, were received. On the 12th the Battalion was put at six hours' notice, and on the 14th came the order to move. The long years of preparation and waiting were at an end.

II

NORMANDY

'ALL ranks of the Battalion were allowed out in the town of Bexhill-on-Sea until 2200 hrs (14th June). Those that had made friends with the local inhabitants gave parties to bid them farewell, while others visited the public houses to drink their last glass of English beer' [1].

The Battalion was to sail in two parts, the marching party from Southampton and the vehicle party from Tilbury. The marching party left Bexhill on 0940 hrs on the 15th, embarked at Southampton at 1200 hrs on the 19th, lay for four days in the gale off Spithead, and landed at 0400 hrs on the 23rd June on the beach at Le Hamel, at the very spot where the 1st Dorsets had carried out the assault landing on D-Day.

The journey of the vehicle party was attended by rather more incident. It left Bexhill, under command of Major L. J. Wood, at 0230 hrs on the 15th, and at 0900 hrs on the 16th reached the transit camp East of London, having had a wonderful reception from the Londoners who threw cigarettes, buns and chocolates into the vehicles[2]; it immediately settled down hoping to make up lost sleep, but actually made its first acquaintance with the 'V-1'[3].

At 1700 hrs on the 17th the party embarked at Tilbury and sailed the same night. After being shelled heavily and continuously from the French coast while travelling between Dover and Folkestone on the 19th, it anchored about 3,000 yards off Arromanches on the 20th. 'The harbour was packed with all classes of ships, corvettes, destroyers, motor torpedo boats, mine sweepers, assault landing craft, floating docks and liberty boats . . . Most of us managed to sleep in our hammocks, but several of us were

[1]Caines [2]Wood [3]Caines

disturbed when a few enemy planes flew over the beach and machine-gunned some of the boats in the harbour. The anti-aircraft fire put up against them was terrific... Iron rations were becoming very short, so we were rationed to one tin of bully beef and a packet of biscuits between two, issued twice daily... A dead body floated alongside our boat, and later another... Through glasses one could see shells bursting on the beaches, lamps signalling and vehicles moving along the coast road'[4].

Most of the party landed on the 22nd, but some had to remain on board for another three days. 'There was a very fed-up feeling among the boys, there being little or no entertainment other than to amuse themselves by playing cards for French francs... Rations were now cut down to almost nothing, a couple of mugs of tea, a tiny piece of corned beef, and a few biscuits. This, I thought, was enough to make any man cry, but we very soon forgot our small problems when German aircraft appeared on the scene; then it was a hell of an exciting time, but never once did they succeed in sinking one single ship'[5]. These remnants landed on the morning of the 25th, and by the afternoon the whole Battalion had concentrated in a field East of Planet, about a mile from the coast, and due North of Bayeux.

On the 26th, in heavy rain, the Battalion arrived at its concentration area between Saint-Gabriel and Vienne-en-Bassin, about six miles due East of Bayeux and about four behind the front line, and at 1300 hrs. on the 28th relieved the Canadian Régiment de la Chaudière in the rear area of Putot-en-Bessin, about half way between Bayeux and Caen. While there, the news was received that Major P. J. Riddle, who had recently left the Battalion to join the 214th Brigade, had been killed[6].

On the 28th the Battalion was put at half an hour's notice to move to the area of the Odon bridgehead. On the morning of the 29th 'we were all beginning to settle down to soldiering, having learned what we thought war was like'[7], but in the early afternoon the Battalion moved to Cheux, about six miles West of Caen and three North of the river. This area had been the scene

[4]Caines [5]Ibid [6]Symonds [7]Caines

of severe fighting, and the fields were strewn with dead and dying cattle and horses. The weather was very close and the smell was quite sickening. Such cows as were still alive had not been milked for a long time[8].

The Battalion arrived in the area at 1840 hrs and almost immediately found out what war was really like, for the 5th D.C.L.I. was having difficulty in repelling an enemy counter-attack supported by tanks, and the C.O. placed B and C Companies under D.C.L.I. command, holding A and D in reserve in the area of Le Haut du Bosq, about half a mile to the South, as a counter-attack force to work with a squadron of Churchill tanks. The fog of war was thick and there was little reliable information as to the whereabouts of the enemy; at 2000 hrs parties of Royal Scots and Royal Scots Fusiliers began to move into the Battalion area from the South and tank squadrons of the 11th Armoured Division formed up on the high ground to the South of the village and moved South-Westwards towards Noyers.

At 2200 hrs A and D Companies were ordered to double up with their respective companies of the D.C.L.I., and the C.O., Lieut.-Colonel H. E. Cowie, went forward to find that the survivors of the Royal Scots and Royal Scots Fusiliers were astride the road about half a mile North of Grainville-sur-Odon, and that they had the situation well in hand. The 4th Dorset area was fairly heavily shelled during the night, but the men were well dug in and suffered few casualties[9].

At 0130 hrs on the 30th the 5th D.C.L.I. moved out of Cheux and the 4th Dorsets took over the area, into which the 7th Hampshires and the 5th Dorsets began to arrive at 1100 hrs. A few German prisoners were taken, but the day was a quiet one apart from enemy shelling. At 1100 hrs on the 1st July, the enemy again started to attack with artillery, but the attempt to break through was stopped by the forward troops, and the Battalion was not engaged, though it captured four enemy snipers. There was heavy rain all night[10].

On the 2nd the Battalion was ordered to be ready to move in

[8]Symonds [9]Cowie [10]Caines

four hours; it was relieved that night. It moved out in heavy rain, and before midnight concentrated in the area of La Gaule, about a mile to the North-East. It remained in this position for two days, suffered some casualties from enemy shelling on the 3rd[11], and had its first bath since leaving England on the 4th[12].

The Battalion moved again on the night of the 5th, and by 0045 hrs on the 6th had relieved a battalion of the Herefords in a defensive position at Tourmauville in the extreme South of the salient across the River Odon; at that time this was the most advanced position in the sector, and the Battalion had the enemy on two flanks[13]. It suffered slight casualties from enemy mortaring. Offensive patrolling began immediately and was maintained throughout the 7th, on which day Cpl. Snooks showed great bravery by going into an anti-personnel minefield to rescue three wounded men[14].

In the late afternoon of the 7th a relief 'recce' party of the Royal Scots arrived, and during the morning the Battalion moved to the rest area of Le Mesnil-Patry, five or six miles behind the firing line, where it remained for two days.

Cheux had given the Battalion its first taste of fire; it was now to fight its first major engagement, and to play its part in the great battle that was being fought for the possession of Caen. At 0115 hrs on the 10th it concentrated at Tourville, on the North bank of the Odon, in preparation for the attack on Eterville, and at 1530 hrs crossed the river and moved to an area immediately East of Miebord, suffering from enemy mortar fire on the way. The Brigade attack was opened by the 5th Dorsets, who captured Fontaine-Etoupefour, half a mile to the West of Eterville: later the 7th Hampshires were sent to capture Maltot, about a mile to the South[15]. Just before the attack on Eterville started, Typhoon fighters rocketed a small wood just in front of the objective[16], and at 0620 hrs the 4th Dorsets' attack was opened by A and B Companies, on the right and left respectively, C and D being held in reserve.

Major Symonds has written the following account of the battle:

[11]Caines [12]Ibid [13]Symonds [14]Cowie [15]Caines [16]Ibid

'Eterville is a small village situated in the high undulating land South of Caen, between the Rivers Odon and Orne. It is surrounded by trees, and was easily identifiable from air photographs, although it was too deep in enemy territory for us to be able to see it before the attack began. The intervening country was principally under high standing corn, which made it difficult to pick out enemy positions, but afforded considerable cover for infantry. All this high ground, which lay to the South of Caen, was very strongly held by the Germans with several Panzer divisions, and was in fact Rommel's hinge position.

'The principal object of our attack was to contain as many enemy as possible in this sector, whilst the Americans were breaking out further West. The supporting fire programme was very heavy and included the R.A.F. and units of the Fleet firing from the Channel. B Company, which I was commanding, was supported by a squadron of Churchill tanks, and A Company by a troop of flame-throwers.

'We began our approach march about midnight on the 9th July, and arrived in the forward assembly area in the early morning, where we had a breakfast of bully beef and biscuits, and checked over our weapons, etc., although there was in fact little left to do, as we had been preparing for this very occasion for so long. Everyone was in high spirits, although of course a little apprehensive, as was only natural in such surroundings as dead and rotting men and animals and destroyed farmsteads all round.

'We formed up immediately behind the start line in a corn field and were shelled a little whilst doing so, causing one or two minor casualties. Colonel Cowie gave the long awaited signal to go by having L/Cpl. Butt sound the charge on his bugle. The Battalion rose to its feet as one man, many cheered. It was a wonderful experience, and we were all glad at that moment to be there.

'As we breasted the top of the hill we overran a German platoon dug in in the corn immediately in front of my company. They offered practically no resistance, surrendering immediately, and we continued the advance to the edge of the village, where we had

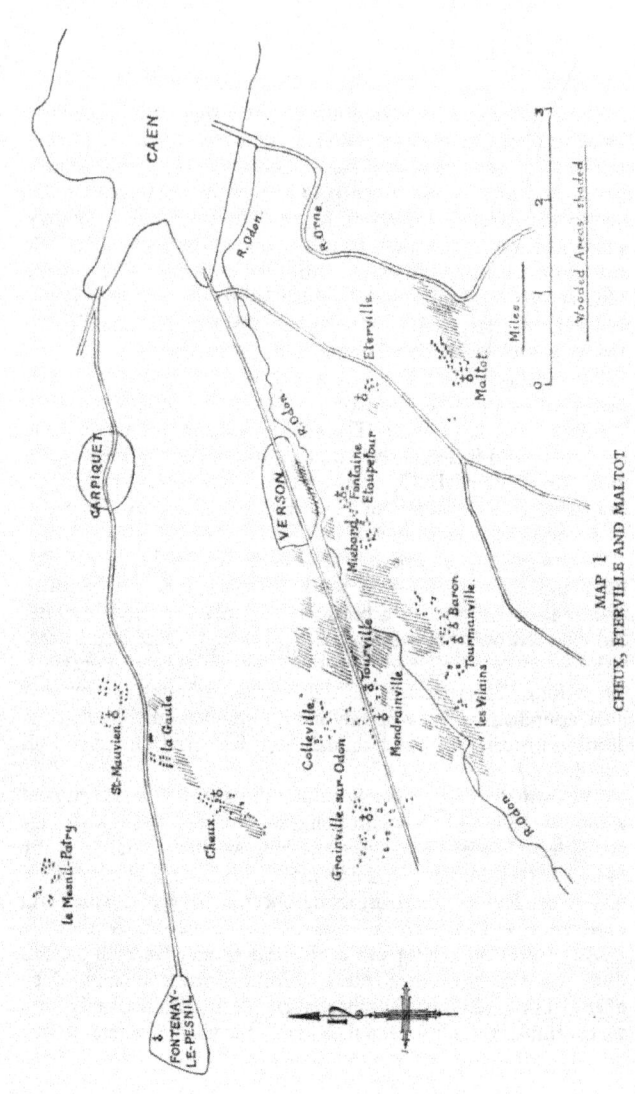

MAP 1
CHEUX, ETERVILLE AND MALTOT

to lie down and wait for the Artillery and the R.A.F. to cease shelling and bombing Eterville. We were very close to the barrage, and still in excellent formation, having suffered only a few casualties from enemy shelling during the advance up to this time.

'The end of the supporting fire was marked by blue smoke shells, and I gave the signal to assault as soon as these fell. No sooner had we begun the assault than about four fighters came over, presumably a little late, and dropped two bombs in the middle of my company whilst we were still in the open field. We could see the bombs falling so had time to lie down, but we suffered a number of casualties from these, including Sgt. Fowler, who was killed, and all three of our No. 88 sets were put out of action.

'The weight of the supporting fire had been so great that the enemy offered no resistance at first, the assault coming before he had had time to recover, and we reached our objective, the road beyond the village, without much difficulty. A number of Germans surrendered, some withdrew, and some had yet to be mopped up. The mopping up, which was done by C and D Companies, was not so easy, as the garden and field hedges were high and the foliage thick, and soon some enemy troops, who had been quiet to start with, opened fire on us. The enemy then began to shell and mortar us very heavily, and he kept this up all the time we were consolidating, making the whole job very difficult. The attack had gone quite a long way into the enemy positions and they were now very close to us on our immediate front.

'I could see A Company, under Major Upton, on my right during the advance and assault, and with their Crocodile flame-throwing tanks in action they looked quite irresistible. They reached their objective on our right about the same time as we did, and probably in rather better order, as they did not get the benefit of our own bombs as we did. As A Company was, later in the day, lost almost to a man at Maltot, I did not get the chance to ask any of them details of their battle at Eterville.

'After I had got my company firmly on the ground and had got the carrier round with more ammunition for the platoons, I began to dig my own slit trench. I had only got the top soil removed when one of the hundreds of shells and bombs that were showering upon us tipped me into my own works. I was unconscious through loss of blood for a little while. However, when I came round I was still there, my Canadian second-in-command, Captain Ron With, had stopped the bleeding for me, and I was able to hand over to him the message that I had just received, to go to Battalion Headquarters for orders to attack Maltot almost at once, as the 7th Hampshires had failed to capture it.

'There are probably few people who know just why the 7th Hampshires failed to capture Maltot, but I witnessed one of the reasons. They were due to pass through Eterville to attack Maltot as soon as we were firm in Eterville, and this they did. As soon as they passed through us they ran into the German counter-attack which was forming up about 300 yards beyond Eterville to try and dislodge us. I shall always believe that the 7th Hampshire's attack on Maltot, coming when it did, saved my company from being completely overrun before we were properly dug in.'

The battle for Eterville 'was a big attack ... and it was highly successful. The 4th Dorsets attacked with great dash, mopped up the village of Eterville, and captured seventy prisoners ...'[17]. For his part in the attack, Major Symonds was awarded the Military Cross. 'By his personal example under shell fire, and in the face of the enemy he proved himself to be a real leader, and he continued to inspire and cheer his men even after he was badly wounded'[18].

'There is no doubt that the whole operation at Eterville was quite a model attack against quite a strong enemy. Although the village was in the front line and a key point in this vital sector, it was held by various battalions quite successfully during the whole of the following fortnight, during which time almost every acre of this high land between the two rivers was severely contested'[19].

The attack had started at 0620 hrs ; by 0745 hrs the objective was taken. 'Everyone dug like hell ... All we had with us was an

[17]Cowie [18]Citation [19]Symonds

entrenching tool, which proved useless; however, to speed up the digging several of us sifted the earth out with our bare hands ... I dug like I had never dug the allotment before'[20].

After consolidating the position and digging in, the Battalion was subjected to heavy enemy mortaring and shelling, and suffered many casualties[21], including Major Symonds and Major Gay, commanding D Company[22]. Captain Baker of the Anti-Tank Platoon, with one leg completely smashed, somehow managed to drive a carrier back to the First Aid Post with other wounded[23]. The Padre went out to find a German M.O., who attended to the enemy wounded and helped to attend to ours[24], and the Battalion M.O., Captain Thompson, was awarded the Military Cross for his courage in looking after the wounded under heavy shell fire[25].

At 1345 hrs the 4th Dorsets were relieved by a battalion of the Cameronians, and reorganised in order to help the 7th Hampshires, who had suffered heavy casaulties at Maltot. 'Several dead Germans lay around, one of which I shall always remember. As I was just sitting down, being practically exhausted ... I saw beneath some long grass a dead Jerry. At first he looked alive, his face seemed to have plenty of colour and his body showed no distinctive markings of death. I was really afraid to touch him or go any nearer him, knowing too well what might happen, for we had all been well drilled as to the possibility of dead bodies being booby traps. Grenades were stuck in his belt, his rifle in his hand and his helmet was still on his head, he had washed and shaved. I kept wondering: eventually I bucked up my courage and touched him to make sure that he was a dead one. Yes, he was all right, but whether he was booby trapped or not, I did not bother to find out'.[26]

At 1600 hrs. the attack on Maltot began, supported by tanks, against terrific opposition from a Panzer division. 'The main body of tactical H.Q. moved on towards the village and was crossing a cornfield on the outskirts. Jerry must have been observing every move, and allowed us to come right up close, thus

[20]Caines [21]Cowie [22]Whittle [23]Ibid [24]Caines [25]Cowie [26]Caines

cutting us off. Suddenly the whole party was cut down by a burst of fire from a Spandau. It was hell, none dared to put his head above the corn, as soon as Jerry observed the slightest movement a burst of fire would be the reply. This firing kept up for some time, everything seemed to open together, self-propelled guns fired practically unceasingly'.[27]

Major Whittle has written the following account of the attack:

'We reorganised in the area known as Horsehoe Wood to the West of Eterville. The information concerning the 7th Hampshires was very vague, and it was not certain whether some of them were still fighting in or near Maltot.

'At 1600 hrs. the attack began. We still had our squadron of Churchill tanks in support, but owing to the position of the 7th Hampshires there was no artillery support initially. The ground was flatish, and the fields were filled with high standing corn; I remember moving forward in my carrier with the corn almost level with the sides, and wishing it were much higher!

'Approaching the village, we came under very heavy machine-gun and anti-tank-gun fire; the enemy had a large number of tanks and self-propelled guns dug in in concealed positions in the orchards and woods surrounding the village. We suffered heavy casualties and many of our tanks were knocked out. As far as I know, all our Anti-Tank Platoon guns were destroyed before they had a chance to go into action.

'The rifle companies and Carrier Platoon all reached their objective, and began to consolidate, by 1645 hrs.

'The next two or three hours were very unpleasant. We had failed to knock out the majority of the dug-in tanks, and in the partly wooded area they were very difficult to locate; the few Churchills remaining with us were withdrawn, and fighting was going on all the time. Battalion Headquarters lost contact with all the rifle companies, and eventually at 2030 hrs there was a small party, consisting of the C.O., Battalion Headquarters, parts of B, C and D Companies, and the Carrier Platoon, dug in on the Northern outskirts of the village. We were under heavy direct

[27]Caines

fire from several of the dug-in tanks. Extremely accurate artillery support was put down by the 112th Field Regiment.

'The C.O. reluctantly gave the order to withdraw, and we passed back through the 7th Somersets and took up a position in the area of Horsehoe Wood. During the withdrawal I went back with R.S.M. Drew to help to bring in a private soldier who had had a foot blown right off, and who up till then had been hopping along on his rifle; he remained quite conscious and cheerful until we got him to an M.O.; only then did he pass out.

'The attack on Maltot had accounted for the whole of A Company, of which not one member returned, and for two-thirds of the other three companies. Major Upton, Major Connor and Major Dawson, commanding A, C and D Companies respectively, were all missing. It was subsequently learned that a large number of the missing were taken prisoner during the night.

'I have a vivid recollection of the efficiency of the German medical personnel whom we captured, who worked hard at bringing in our wounded as well as their own before and after our First Aid Post was established.

'We spent the night of the 10th/11th July in a position just forward of Horsehoe Wood. The Battalion strength that night was five officers, including the C.O., and less than eighty other ranks; this, of course, does not include the L.O.B.'s and the échelons.'

'As dawn broke (on the 11th) every man stood to in his newly dug slit trench, ready to deal with the expected assault from the enemy. It was considered that Jerry had possibly reorganised his troops during the night and would assault in the morning. All of us were cold as stones, extremely worn out and dog tired . . . I myself felt fit to drop, it had been a terrible twenty-four hours, something I will never forget as long as I live, seeing men fall, and hearing the wounded cry and moan with pain as they were evacuated. I could never express in my own words the horror experienced on this day'.[28]

But the expected attack did not come, and at 0530 hrs on the

[26]Caines

11th the Battalion again moved forward to take up a position half way between Fontaine and Maltot, which had been recaptured by the Germans, and remained there until relieved by the 5th Dorsets in the evening, when it went to reorganise in the area of Colleville, North of the River Odon.

It spent three days re-equipping at Colleville, which 'proved to be smack in the middle of a gun area, and we were continually catching some of the counter-battery fire. There were several casualties, two of whom were the M.O. and the Padré, who were both wounded.

'We were reinforced by small parties from several different regiments; a large contingent from the Essex Regiment, including some officers, went "en bloc" to form a completely new A Company. Captain Roper and Captain Letson were both promoted to Major and took over C and D Companies. I took over S Company.'[29]

At 2315 hrs on the 14th the Battalion, now commanded by Lieut.-Colonel L. J. Wood, returned to Maltot, relieving the 1st Worcesters in the line about one mile to the North-West of the village.

'We moved into a defensive position overlooking Maltot, in the area of the Château de Fontaine, to the South-West of Eterville. The position was on a forward slope, and we were continually being mortared and shelled; no movement was possible during daylight, and supplies and ammunition were brought up each night. There were numerous dead cattle in the fields and many dead Germans in the hedges, and the stench was foul.'[30]

The Battalion remained in this position until the 18th and had a particularly unpleasant time, as enemy mortaring and shelling were constant, and there was a large number of casualties. Active patrolling was carried out every night, very good work being done by Captain Hall and Lieuts. Hodges and Cottle.[31]

'During this period a prisoner was taken who turned out to be a German Pay Corps N.C.O., and he had a considerable sum of money in Reichsmarks on him. He was apparently making the

[29] Whittle [30] Ibid [31] Wood

MR. MACKENZIE KING INTRODUCES GENERAL SMUTS TO CANADIAN OFFICERS SERVING WITH THE 4TH BATTALION THE DORSET REGIMENT. 12.5.44

THE CARRIER PLATOON OF THE 4TH BATTALION THE DORSET REGIMENT CROSSING THE PONTOON BRIDGE ACROSS THE SEINE. PICTURE TAKEN FROM VERNONNET. 27.8.44

rounds of the forward positions, and had ventured a little too far forward.'[32] As a result of his indiscretion more than 23,900 francs went to the regimental prisoner-of-war fund[33].

'One night an enemy plane dropped a bomb about thirty yards from S Company Headquarters, and the new Anti-Tank Platoon commander, who was with me in my trench, was hit in the chest; he had arrived only about thirty minutes earlier.'[34]

On the 18th the C.O. was wounded in the head by a mortar bomb; he was evacuated but returned a few days later[35], and in the meantime the second-in-command, Major Tilly, assumed command. At 2200 hrs the same day the Battalion was obliged to take up a new position three hundred yards to the rear, where it remained until the 26th. 'During this period we witnessed a huge daylight bomber force putting down a carpet about one mile in front of our positions; it was an awe-inspiring sight.'[36]

Except for the capture of Eterville, which deserves to rank high in the annals of the Regiment, and the subsequent heavy fighting at Maltot, the 4th Dorsets played no part in the fighting for Caen, and on the afternoon of the 26th July moved into the rest area of Condé-sur-Seulles, about six miles South-East of Bayeux. On its arrival the Battalion received its first hot meal for many days, as all the time it had been in the Fontaine-Maltot sector each man had been obliged to cook for himself on a Tommy cooker.[37] 'I shall never forget the sight the men looked when they returned, dirty, muddy clothes, and hardly a man had shaved in eight days, but they were all on top of form, they arrived singing popular songs, and all had the usual wisecrack.'[38] The three days at Condé were mainly spent in cleaning up, re-equipping and reorganising; the Divisional Commander visited the Brigade and congratulated it on its performance[39], and there was a certain amount of recreation: an E.N.S.A. show visited the camp,[40] and the men were given an opportunity of visiting Bayeux.[41]

---

[32]Whittle [33]*Western Gazette* [34]Whittle [35]Ibid [36]Ibid [37]Caines [38]Ibid [39]Wood [40]Caines [41]Wood

III

THE BREAK-THROUGH AND THE PURSUIT

It was intended that the Battalion should rest for ten days at Condé,[1] but events made that impossible. The capture of the Faubourg de Vaucelles, the part of Caen South of the River Orne, completed the break-through along the whole of the Allied line,[2] and on the 29th July the 4th Dorsets left Condé for the area of Couvigny-Le Repas, about two miles North-East of Caumont, where they arrived in the late afternoon. With the 5th Dorsets on its left,[3] the Battalion was ordered to attack the hamlet of La Londe with a squadron of tanks under command and full artillery support.[4]

At 0920 hrs on the 30th the Battalion moved up to the start line, but at 1000 hrs the attack was postponed and the Battalion waited all day in position for it to begin, suffering from constant mortaring and a fair amount of shelling.[5] At 1800 hrs the attack was cancelled and the 7th Hampshires were ordered to attack La Londe from the flank[6], while the 4th Dorsets concentrated for the night some four hundred yards behind the start line.

During the night orders were received to clear the ground in front of the 5th Dorsets, whose progress was impeded by a large number of the enemy[7], and at 0500 hrs on the 31st the 4th Dorsets moved forward to Montmirel, about one mile East of Caumont, and dug in. The C.O. decided to move round by the West and to make the attack due East, thus moving across the front of the 5th Dorsets on the left, the right being protected by the 7th Hampshires, who had captured La Londe and advanced

[1]Wood [2]Eisenhower [3]Hartwell [4]Wood [5]Ibid [6]Ibid [7]Ibid

beyond it[8]. At 0900 hrs patrols of A Company, commanded by Major Grafton, were sent South to the orchards surrounding La Londe, and at 1500 hrs the main body of the Battalion started the attack from Montmirel. It went exceptionally well and in about four hours the objective was taken, as well as eighty-seven prisoners, for the cost of half a dozen casualties. The Pioneer Platoon, under Sergt. Blandemer, did excellent work in clearing anti-personnel minefields[9].

The Battalion was immediately ordered to swing South to capture Point 174 on the ridge South-East of Caumont[10], and in the heat of a gruelling afternoon it moved forward to its new objective, which it captured without opposition. Here it dug in for the night[11], which 'was remarkable for the fact that no firing of any sort took place and that the quietness was quite uncanny'[12]. Patrols were sent forward all night long and returned with a few prisoners[13].

The Battalion stayed in its new position throughout the 1st August, when mortaring was fairly constant[14]. 'The weather was still blisteringly hot ... Several dead animals, victims of the shelling, lay around the whole area we were occupying ... The stink was terrible, especially during the night after a hot day, the dead animals were literally running with maggots and flies'[15].

That evening the C.O. was informed that the Division was to make a break-out on the road Caumont-Cahagnes-Jurques-Ondefontaine: the 130th Brigade was to move that night, and the 4th Dorsets were to lead the attack with a squadron of Sherman tanks, a section of R.E., a platoon of anti-tank guns and a platoon of medium machine-guns under command. Their task was to seize Jurques, La Bigne and Ondefontaine; the capture of La Bigne was essential, but if the Battalion suffered heavy casualties there, another battalion would pass through to take Ondefontaine[16]. It was anticipated that the Battalion would cover twenty miles without meeting any enemy[17], an estimate that turned out to be incorrect.

[8]Wood [9]Ibid [10]Ibid [11]W.D. [12]Wood [13]Caines [14]Wood [15]Caines [16]Wood [17]Caines

The Battalion and its supporting arms[18] concentrated at 2330 hrs. 'As we formed up along the side of the road, enemy aircraft dropped parachute flares and illuminated the area completely; they followed up with anti-personnel bombs, but were well off their target'[19]. At 0115 hrs on the 2nd the Battalion moved off South-Westwards at a steady pace, the Carrier Platoon leading[20]. 'It was a terrible night, troops were lifted on tanks, and were continually dropping off to sleep'[21]. 'I was leading the column in a carrier driven by Pte. Brake. It was pitch dark and we had no idea what we might run into. On approaching Cahagnes we saw a light flicker and went forward on foot to find one of the Divisional M.P.'s there at the cross-roads: he was under the impression that he was in Caumont. We came upon two Tiger tanks on the road; they caused a lot of excitement before we discovered them to be abandoned'[22].

At 0915 hrs A Company, the leading company, was within half a mile of Jurques and encountered mines. 'The road was heavily cratered and while we were searching for mines a machine-gun opened up on us'[23]. Patrols pushed forward and met opposition for the first time. 'A few fanatics were holding out in the village itself. These fools were quickly dealt with, and were no more'[24]. 'At this point the Adjutant, Captain Goddard, in trying to catch up with the column, took a different route and entered Jurques in front of us. We heard an explosion and pushed forward, and half way between Jurques and La Bigne we found the Adjutant's scout car blown up on a mine. Captain Goddard had been killed outright, and Lieut. Bogan, the Signals Officer, was badly burned'[25].

Between Jurques and La Bigne, a couple of miles further on, the country was hilly and very close, and afforded excellent positions for the enemy to delay the advance from the front and flanks. The road was mined, and while the Sappers and the Battalion Pioneers were clearing it, the column was engaged by fire from the flank[26]. 'The Battalion passed through Jurques fairly easily, but as soon

[18]Wood [19]Whittle [20]Ibid [21]Caines [22]Whittle [23]Ibid [24]Caines [25]Whittle [26]Wood

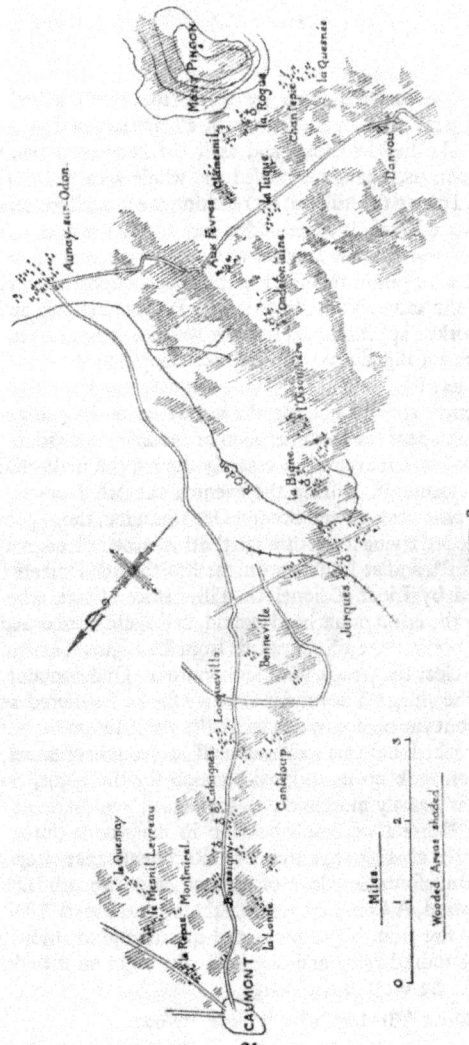

MAP 2

CAUMONT, ONDEFONTAINE AND MONT PINCON

Point 174, and the road Caumont–Cahagnes–Jurgues–Ondefontaine are not shown. See p. 19

as we left the battered town we were faced with a hell of a resistance; Jerry then opened up with all he had, self-propelled guns fired like hell let loose, and as if the heavens above were opening upon us, Spandaus rattled the whole area'[27]. 'A' Company moved on up the hill, but on reaching the top, a few hundred yards from La Bigne, it came under very heavy fire and suffered heavy casualties. It made another attempt to go forward, and the C.O. decided to put in two more companies, supported by tanks, as soon as the mines were cleared. The Pioneer Platoon and the Sappers worked splendidly; the attack was not long delayed, and by 1600 hrs La Bigne was captured and mopping-up operations were completed[28].

The enemy was still holding the woods beyond La Bigne, so the Battalion spent the late afternoon of the 2nd consolidating its position, and was mortared incessantly during the night and the following morning[29]. During the evening the 5th Dorsets were ordered to pass through and occupy Ondefontaine; they spent the whole of the 3rd trying to get through the thick wood through which the road ran[30], and at 1400 hrs on the 3rd the 4th Dorsets (now commanded by Lieut.-Colonel G. Tilly, since Wood, who was still feeling the effect of his head wound, had again been evacuated the day before) attacked Southwards from La Bigne. Their intention was to clear the woods West and South of Ondefontaine and to occupy the village. They ran into heavy fire and suffered severe casualties, but the objective was gained[31]. At 1615 hrs the enemy counter-attacked, but this was beaten off in a couple of hours, and the Battalion took up its original position for the night, during which it was heavily mortared and shelled.

The 5th Dorsets were still held up in the woods during the 4th August[32]; at 1700 hrs the 43rd Reconnaissance Regiment reported Ondefontaine clear of enemy, and the 4th Dorsets moved forward, A Company leading the attack, but at 1830 hrs, stopped by fire from Tiger tanks and machine-guns, they withdrew four hundred yards and dug in for the night on the edge of the wood to the West of the village.

[27]Caines [28]Wood [29]Ibid [30]Ibid [31]Whittle [32]Wood

Ondefontaine was heavily mortared and shelled during the night, and at 0500 hrs on the 5th, the 4th Dorsets entered the village[33], of which there was literally nothing left[34], the enemy having completely withdrawn during the night.

The 6th was spent at Ondefontaine, resting and clearing up, and at 1100 hrs on the 7th the Battalion went forward again to occupy Clamesnil and a small bridge about a quarter of a mile to the South-East. By 1500 hrs Clamesnil was clear of the enemy, and the Battalion was informed that it was to have a two days' rest. 'By 2200 hrs all had dug in well ... I had managed also to strip off and wash down, but just as several of us were naked over came a stonk of shells—talk about being caught with one's trousers down, we certainly were'[35].

But the hope of two days' rest proved illusory, for that very evening the Battalion was ordered to move at once to relieve the 6th K.R.R.C. in the area of Danvou, prior to playing an inconspicuous part in the capture of Mont Pinçon, one of the 43rd Division's major exploits in the campaign. In order to block any possible move South by the enemy from Aunay, the 5th Dorsets had already taken up a position round La Roguerie, at the Western foot of this steep and commanding hill[36], and at 0100 hrs on the 8th the 4th Dorsets arrived in the area of Duval-Chantepie, about one mile to the West of it and the same distance North of Danvou, where it prepared to meet an enemy counter-attack that never came. At 0830 hrs patrols went out to investigate Danvou, and at 1500 hrs two platoons advanced to the château and cleared the position.

The Battalion held the same positions throughout the 9th, and carried out active patrolling all day[37] in blistering heat[38]. Captain Andrews, a Canadian who had formerly been the Battalion's Intelligence Officer, was killed while looking for a man who had not returned from a patrol, and was awarded a posthumous Military Cross for his gallantry. He had been very popular and was mourned by the whole Battalion[39]. By the end of the morning two companies of the 5th Dorsets were established on the hill,

[33]W.D. [34]Caines [35]Ibid [36]Hartwell [37]W.D. [38]Caines [39]Ibid

which was captured later in the day by the 129th Brigade, assisted by a diversionary attack by the 7th Hampshires[40].

The 10th was spent fairly quietly in the same positions, and early on the 11th came the order to move. By this time such of the German Army as remained West of the Seine had been bottled up in a pocket whose mouth had been narrowed down to the gap—about twenty miles wide—between Argentan and Falaise, and the task of the 43rd Division was to apply pressure to the North-Western edge of the pocket. The 4th Dorsets were ordered to attack Le Fresnes, about three miles East of Condé-sur-Noireau[41], while the 5th Dorsets were to capture Proussy, about two and a half miles to the North of it[42].

The Battalion left Danvou at 0800 hrs on the 13th, but at 1130 hrs. it was held up on its line of advance by an enemy counter-attack on the 129th Brigade. It pushed forward to a line about two miles East of Saint-Pierre-La-Vieille and took up a defensive position[43], where it was fairly frequently shelled, but suffered few casualties[44].

The 5th Dorsets started their successful attack on Proussy at 0630 hrs on the 14th[45], and at 1230 hrs the 4th Dorsets moved to their concentration area half a mile to the North. At 1700 hrs the attack on Le Fresnes began, against slight enemy shelling. 'Several of the local French inhabitants came out to cheer us on to the objective; they threw flowers down at our feet and offered us gallons of cider, which was accepted by many of us thirsty fellows'[46]. The attack met with very little opposition, and by 2200 hrs Le Fresnes was captured at the cost of two casualties. 'Many p.w. were captured, all seemed fully prepared to give themselves up. Some of them were a pitiful sight to see, they looked unshaven, hungry and very badly clothed'[47]. Point 201, on the Southern edge of the village, being the highest hill for miles around, the position was very exposed, so the Battalion dug in. The night passed without incident except for odd parties of

[40]Hartwell [41]W.D. [42]Hartwell [43]W.D. [44]Caines [45]Hartwell [46]Caines [47]Ibid

Germans who crept out from behind hedgerows to give themselves up, and who appeared only too willing to do so[48].

The next five days were spent clearing up and resting. On the 19th the Battalion was visited by an E.N.S.A. show and a mobile

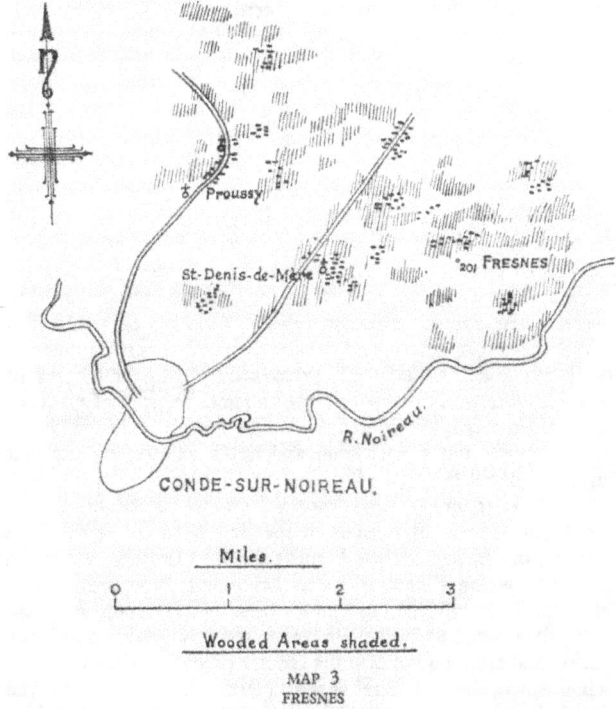

MAP 3
FRESNES

bath unit. 'All of us had heard of mobile bath units before, but considered them as something written on paper for higher commanders to see. All we needed was bath salts to finish the job

[48]Caines

off'[49]. Here also the Battalion made the acquaintance of 'Calvados', the very potent local brew of potato whisky[50].

On the 20th the Battalion moved to a concentration area North of La Lande-Saint-Siméon, about four miles South-East of Condé, and spent the next day there.

On the 20th the Falaise gap was closed at Chambois, and on the 22nd the pocket was eliminated altogether[51]; the next task before the Allies was to pursue them to and across the Seine, and on the British front the 43rd Division was given the honour of making the assault crossing. At 1300 hrs on the 22nd the Battalion left its concentration area and travelled all day and all night through Falaise, Argentan, L'Aigle and Evreux to Saint-Illiers-La-Ville, about four miles West of the river, where it arrived at 1045 hrs on the 23rd. The journey was made with no delays more serious than those imposed by mines and a blown bridge, but was not without some gruesome interest, for the road ran right through the heart of the Falaise-Argentan pocket. 'We were now well into where mass slaughters had taken place by Typhoon fighter-bombers ... and actually our vehicles travelled over the top of many hundreds of crushed German bodies. Vehicles of all types of German transport littered the whole area ... This road was about a mile and a half long, and never before have I smelt anything like it'[52].

At 1315 hrs on the same day the Battalion moved on foot to Le Mesnil-Simon, five miles to the South, where, apart from sending out 'recce' parties, it spent the 24th resting, 'We met a charming young French girl with her mother who came out to greet us. They informed us that we were the first troops they had seen, they asked us into their house, gave us flowers and black coffee, and after a quiet chat the mother produced a bottle of rich wine, which, she said, as far as we understood, that she had saved for their day of liberation. After a few drinks and having done our business, we returned to the Battalion feeling quite well satisfied. Our vehicles were all decorated with bunches of flowers'[53].

[49]Caines [50]Whittle [51]Eisenhower [52]Caines [53]Ibid

The task of the 43rd Division was to cross the Seine from Vernon and to capture the high ground immediately opposite the town on the right bank of the river. At 1830 hrs on the 24th the Battalion was put at two hours' notice to move to Vernon, and at 1600 hrs on the 25th it left Le Mesnil and started towards its destination by an extremely devious route. 'As we travelled through various French villages the local civilian population came running out throwing flowers on the ground in front of us, and whenever we stopped we were offered cider'[54]. At 0830 hrs on the 26th the Battalion concentrated North of Gauciel, about four miles East of Evreux; the forward troops had reached the left bank of the Seine the day before[55], and at Gauciel the terrific rumble of the British artillery, firing in support of the Brigade that was about to assault, was distinctly audible[56].

At 0650 hrs on the 27th the Battalion left in transport for Vernon. At 1230 hrs enemy aircraft succeeded in damaging the pontoon bridge which the Sappers had just finished constructing, but repairs were completed by 1530 hrs, and by 1600 hrs the whole Battalion was across[57] and in the bridgehead that had been captured by the other two Brigades of the Division[58]. By 1630 hrs the Battalion had concentrated on the high ground one mile East of the river, after some opposition from enemy machine-guns.

The axis for the break-out was the road leading North-East from Vernon through Gisors to Beauvais[59]. Throughout the night a continuous stream of traffic crossed the river to reinforce the bridgehead[60], and during the night orders were given for every single battalion in the Division to attack in the morning, to enlarge the bridgehead, put the Germans to rout, and gain the thickly wooded high ground on both sides of the road[61]; the 4th Dorsets were ordered to capture the high ground and houses one mile short of the village of Tilly, while the 5th Dorsets were to capture the hamlet of La Queue d'Haye to its right. Heavy rain had soaked everyone to the skin[62], and under these conditions the

[54]Caines [55]Ibid [56]Ibid [57]W.D. [58]Hartwell [59]Ibid [60]Ibid [61]Caines [62]Ibid

Battalion started to attack at 0900 hrs on the 28th. No real opposition was encountered[63], but owing to the bad weather and the density of the woods progress was slow[64], and it was not until 1540 hrs that Tilly was captured by the 7th Hampshires, who swept onto it from the right.

On the 29th the Battalion was informed that it was not likely to move for forty-eight hours; it actually stayed where it was for a fortnight since all its transport was commandeered to help in supplying the advancing armoured divisions[65]. During this time it had a well earned rest and a good deal of recreation. On September 2nd the Divisional Commander addressed the Brigade and presented medals; a mobile cinema unit and an E.N.S.A. show visited the area, and parties visited Paris.

By the evening of the 31st August a wide bridgehead had been formed, which allowed the 11th and Guards Armoured Divisions to pass through on their drive into Belgium[66], and by the morning of the 1st September the Battalion was well behind the front line, since the Guards Armoured Division had chased the Germans some forty miles overnight[67]. By the 10th the Battalion was mobile again, and on the morning of the 11th it left Tilly to continue the triumphal progress that had started in Normandy. On the 12th it left France and crossed the frontier into Belgium, where the welcome it got from the Belgians was perhaps even more overwhelming than that of the French during the move to the Seine[68].

The Battalion reached Meerbeke, about fifteen miles West of Brussels, on the afternoon of the 12th, and was billeted in and around the town. It only spent two days there, for there was serious work ahead, but they were festive days: recreational transport was arranged for taking the men into Brussels, where the warmth of the welcome was truly overpowering[69], and a large German wine store was found at Ninove. Thousands of bottles were issued to the Division, and champagne was drunk at breakfast, dinner, tea and supper for many days to come[70].

[63]W.D. [64]Hartwell [65]Caines [66]Hartwell [67]Caines [68]Ibid [69]Hartwell [70]Caines

IV

ARNHEM

By the middle of September the Allied armies in the North were in South Holland and along the frontier between Belgium and Germany, and the Supreme Commander ordered the strongest pressure to be applied in this sector with a view to seizing the bridges over the Rhine, thus turning the German right flank, and opening the road across the North German plain to Berlin. The operation planned for this purpose consisted of two parts: the airborne operation had as its object the capture of the bridges at Grave, Nijmegen and Arnhem on the 17th, while the armoured troops and infantry of the British Second Army were to advance Northwards in support of the airborne troops, pass over the captured bridges, and push on to the Zuider Zee, thus, if successful, cutting off the German troops in Western Holland[1]. The 43rd Division was to follow the Guards Armoured Division, which was to lead the break-out, and to be prepared to make assault crossings of the many waterways in Holland should the bridges be blown. If the airborne troops failed to secure the bridges, it was probable that the 43rd Division would have to make assault crossings both at Nijmegen and Arnhem[2].

On the afternoon of the 14th the Battalion moved from Meerbeke to the village of Hunberg, some five miles North of Diest, where the Brigadier held a conference in the village school and planning for the move into Holland began[3]. The divisional attack was to be led by the 130th Brigade, and the Division's ultimate objective was the capture of the high ground South of Apeldoorn, about sixteen miles North of Arnhem.

On the 17th the Battalion moved to Hechtel, and left again on

[1]Eisenhower [2]Hartwell [3]Ibid

the morning of the 20th. It travelled in D.U.K.W.'s all day and all night, passing through Eindhoven, Tilburg and 's Hertogenbosch, and at 0600 hrs on the 21st the leading company was one mile South-West of Grave, on the River Maas. The Battalion's immediate task was to defend the road bridge at Neder Asselt and the railway bridge over the Maas-Waal Canal two miles South of Nijmegen; civilians had reported enemy units West and South-East of Grave, and the local police had reported enemy tanks four miles South of the town, but no incidents were reported by the companies.

On the 21st the 130th Brigade was ordered to clear Nijmegen, and the 5th Dorsets went in to do it. 'This was quite the most fantastic operation; far from finding any Germans lurking in the town, it was with the greatest difficulty that any progress could be made through the excited inhabitants, who festooned the troops with flowers and filled their pockets with apples'[4].

On the 22nd the 5th Dorsets followed the Guards Armoured Division towards Elst, where the opposition proved too strong for any further advance. The situation of the British Airborne Forces at Arnhem was now critical, and the 130th Brigade was given the task of making contact with them, so that supplies could be ferried across and casualties evacuated[5]. The corridor between Nijmegen and Arnhem was hardly wider than the road connecting them and was cut several times a day, and the fog of war was so dense that on one occasion three Tiger tanks actually joined the British column and took part in the advance[6].

The 4th Dorsets had left Grave on the 22nd, and took up a position immediately East of the Maas-Waal Canal, astride the railway leading into Nijmegen; at 0630 hrs on the 23rd, they moved forward to play their part in the relief of Arnhem. The advance was badly held up owing to the armour in front being stuck, by the heavy rain[7], and by enemy mortaring and sniping,

[4]Hartwell [5]Ibid [6]Caines [7]Ibid. Captain (then Sergt.) Caines was in hospital at this time and did not rejoin the Battalion until October 2nd. The account of the operation given in his diary was received later from Major Hall and Captain Stoddart.

and they did not arrive in the Homoet area, where they had the 7th Hampshires on their left[8], until 1645 hrs.

During the afternoon the 5th Dorsets, with a squadron of the 13/18th Hussars, led the Brigade in a mad dash to Driel, and managed to establish its forward companies on the bank of the Lek opposite Oosterbeek[9], and during the night of the 23rd/24th the Polish Airborne Brigade forced a crossing of the river, but owing to a late start only half of it got over[10].

On the 24th, the 4th Dorsets were ordered to cross at the site of the ferry about a mile and a half West of Oosterbeek, in order to enlarge the bridgehead already held by the Parachutists, and to get supplies across. A and B Companies, commanded by Majors Grafton and Whittle respectively[11], were to lead in the first flight of assault boats, and C and D, commanded by Majors Crocker and Roper[12], were to follow. S Company, with the supplies, was to cross last[13]. The assault, whose objective was a factory some six hundred yards inland[14], was to be supported by three regiments of artillery. It was to start at 2200 hrs.

'During the afternoon the C.O., Lieut.-Colonel Tilley, and the company commanders went forward to Driel, and from the top of the church steeple had a good look at the ferry where the crossing was to be made. The enemy must have realised the value of the steeple as an O.P. and pumped some shells into it while we were there'[15].

At 1930 hrs the Battalion moved off, under murderous fire, with rations and ammunition for four days, and at 2130 hrs arrived at Driel. Owing to the intense enemy fire to which it was subjected throughout the operation, it arrived in scattered parties, and had to form up again, with A Company to the right and B to the left in front, and C to the right and D to the left in the rear. From here to the river bank, everything, including the assault boats[16], had to be carried by hand for some 600 yards, through an orchard and over obstructions. One boat was set on fire and others were holed before they could be got into the water[17].

[8]Caines [9]Hartwell [10]Ibid [11]Whittle [12]Ibid [13]Ibid [14]Caines [15]Whittle [16]Ibid [17]*The Times*

'The assault boats we had been carrying with us had been taken from us the previous night and used in the unsuccessful attempt to cross the river by the Polish Airborne Brigade, who

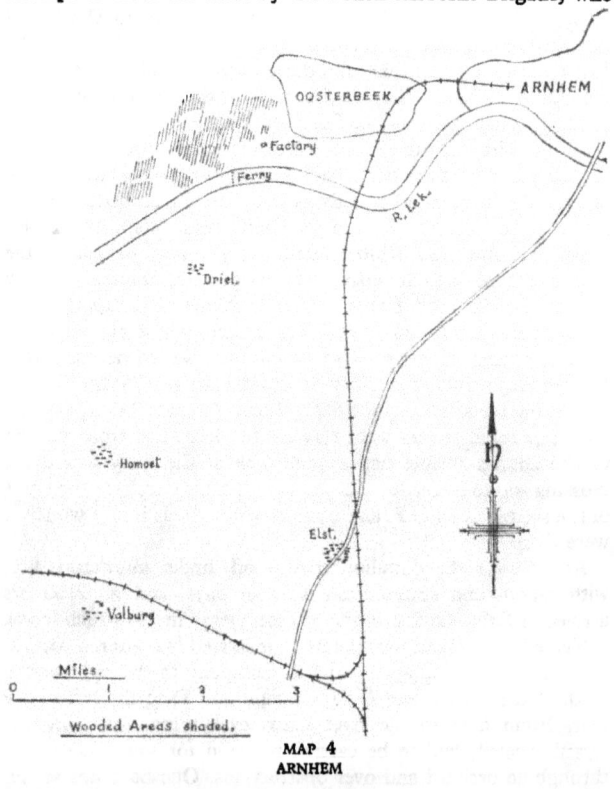

MAP 4
ARNHEM

had dropped on the wrong side of the river. We were therefore ready to go without any means of crossing, and the fresh boats that had been sent off from Division were in a bogged lorry back near Nijmegen. We spent three unpleasant hours waiting, and eventually the boats turned up, due mainly, I believe, to the energy of Captain Dawes of the 5th Dorsets'[18].

At 0100 hrs on the 25th the forward companies moved down to the bank under a heavy artillery barrage[19]; the first flight of boats left for the opposite bank and was immediately engaged by withering fire from the enemy. The crossing continued until 0215 hrs, when it had to be stopped owing to enemy pressure, though later three D.U.K.W.'s managed to get across with supplies. By 0215 hrs it was estimated that 17 officers and 298 other ranks had reached the opposite bank[20], representing the bulk of A and B Companies, Headquarters and one platoon of D Company and Battalion Headquarters[21].

Major Whittle has written the following account of the crossing and of the fighting on the opposite bank:

'The enemy opened up with counter-fire, and at least two of the ten boats in my company group were holed badly before reaching the bank. We were launching the first boat when they opened up with M.M.G. fire from the opposite bank, the boat sank, and we had several casualties. We discovered that this fire was on fixed lines, and by moving a few yards the remainder of the boats were launched successfully.

'There was a strong current, and my two leading boats were swept rapidly towards the West where the factory, about 400 yards down stream, was ablaze, and we should have been beautifully silhouetted. By using spades as well as the quite inadequate paddles we eventually landed about 100 yards East of the factory and got ashore without much trouble.

'We moved forward to the edge of the trees about 50 yards from the river bank and waited for the remainder of the company, but only two further boatloads joined us. It was subsequently discovered that of our ten boats three were holed before launching, one was swept downstream and landed below the burning factory, four crossed with us, and the other two were sunk during

[18]Whitte [19]Ibid [20]W.D. [21]Caines

the crossing. On the spot the strength of B Company was 2 officers and less than 30 other ranks.

'Where the trees started there was a steep bank about 100 feet high, and the enemy were well dug in on the top of it. We started an assault and met very heavy opposition: it was only too easy for the Jerries on top to roll grenades down on us, and we eventually gained the top at the expense of 50 per cent of our strength, for when we occupied the trenches at the top we were reduced to about fifteen. We were joined by the C.O., Major Roper and about twenty men of C Company; they set out to the right to try to contact A Company and ran into opposition almost immediately.'

The C.O.'s party advanced up the wooded slope but was soon surrounded and forced to surrender, the C.O.'s last words being 'There they are, boys: get at them with the bayonet.' Major Roper's party forced its way up the slope and reached the top by dawn, but also found itself completely surrounded. It held out for an hour and a half, and was then forced to surrender[22].

Major Whittle continues:

'After some while I took two men with me and moved off along the top of the bank to try and contact the other companies, leaving the other small group under Lieut. MacDermott. We failed to make any contact but ran into quite a lot of enemy patrols and positions.

'It was now almost light, so we returned to the landing point where I found about twenty others. I called in the remainder of B Company and we searched for any others in the nearby trees, and I gave the order to dig in behind a bank half way between the river and the trees. On checking up I discovered my strength to be about thirty, comprising a few of B, C and D Companies, about ten of S Company and a M.O. and Quartermaster belonging to the Airborne Forces.

'We remained in this position throughout the day. Our trenches were continually being fired on by snipers on the top of the bank among the trees and a German patrol made an attempt

[22]Caines

to attack us. There were several casualties from snipers and M.M.G. fire, and also from a well-meaning couple of Spitfires which "strafed" us. A German speaking reasonably good English did his best to make us surrender.

'After dark that night German patrol activity became very active, and one group was located infiltrating along the river bank behind us. I therefore gave the order to withdraw to the river bank. One man, a strong swimmer, volunteered to try and get back to Brigade Headquarters for further orders. We waited about another hour and a half, during which time we had several skirmishes with enemy patrols, and at about 2300 hrs I decided to withdraw across the river. We had found one sound boat and the wounded and non-swimmers were pushed off in this; the rest of us swam back. I arrived back at Brigade Headquarters in Driel with about fifteen men at 2330 hrs.

'I have little knowledge of the action of the other companies over the river. A Company landed even more scattered than we did and eventually Major Grafton with his F.O.O. and a few men got through to the Airborne bridgehead; they were evacuated with the Airborne Forces. Major Crocker was badly wounded during the landing, and the C.O. and Major Roper were both captured just before dawn.'

The part of the Battalion which had not crossed the river had been occupied during the day in preparing for the withdrawal of the Airborne Forces[23], and at 1500 hrs the order was received that they were to be evacuated across the river during the night, followed by the 4th Dorsets[24]. Major Hall volunteered to cross with orders for the Dorsets[25]; he got across, but was obliged to return without having been able to make any contact with the Battalion[26]. For this action he was awarded the Military Cross. 'Throughout the whole of these two nights he showed an offensive spirit and disregard for his own safety, which were an inspiration to all'[27].

'The tremendous difficulties of the evacuation . . . can hardly be imagined. No lights could be used and the night was so dark

[23]Whittle [24]W.D. [25]Ibid [26]Caines [27]Citation

that men had to walk in front of the vehicles, and even then could scarcely be seen by the drivers. Many vehicles slipped off the narrow roads into the ditch and had to be overturned in order to keep the way clear. Torrential rain was falling the whole time and the enemy continued to harass the area with shell and mortar fire. The guns fired a continuous barrage to cover the evacuation and tracer was used as a directional guide to the boats crossing the river'[28].

The evacuation was due to begin at about 2200 hrs[29], and at 2330 hrs the first small party arrived back in an assault boat. By first light on the 26th, some two thousand of the Airborne Forces had returned, but very few Dorsets; at 2200 hrs. one man from the Airborne Forces swam across and reported that there were still some fifty of the Airborne Forces and some Dorsets on the other bank; a 'recce' boat succeeded in crossing, but only brought back one man from the Dorsets.

It seemed impossible to make any further contact with the cut off forces, and at 0500 hrs on the 27th the Battalion returned to the Homoet area to regroup and refit. At 1750 hrs a few parties crossed the river for the last time[30], largely on improvised rafts[31] and succeeded in bringing back four more Dorset men.

Five more men swam back on the morning of the 28th, but the crossing of the afternoon of the 27th was the last attempt at a rescue, for the initiative, such as it was, had temporarily passed to the enemy. The area was heavily shelled during the six days that the Battalion stayed in it, and on the morning of the 28th a German patrol crossed the river, but was quickly put out of action by the 5th Dorsets[32]. On the 29th orders were issued for meeting an expected counter-attack; it did not come, but the 7th Hampshires reported early on the 1st October that eleven enemy assault boats had crossed the river, and in the afternoon about fifty Germans came over and were quickly dealt with by the 5th Dorsets, this being the prelude to a series of small counter-attacks that were to go on for the rest of the day[33].

The attempt to secure the bridge over the Lek at Arnhem had

[28]Hartwell [29]Ibid [30]W.D. [31]Caines [32]Hartwell [33]Ibid

failed, but the operation, of which Arnhem was an indispensable part, had brought very positive and important advantages to the Allied Forces. It enabled the British and Canadians, pushing Northwards and Westwards, to establish a solid line running along the Waal and the Maas, and the American Northern Group of Armies to expand Eastwards, thus coming into line with the Central Group, and within striking distance of Cleve. The bridgeheads over the Waal and the Maas could be made secure, and the land between the two rivers later served as a valuable corridor for the advance to the Rhine[34].

Accounts of all the acts of individual heroism and initiative performed at Arnhem would be impossible in this brief history, and the following two, for which Cpl. A. C. Smith and Pte. L. Driver were awarded the Military Medal, must serve as being typical of many.

'On the 25th September, 1944, during the assault crossing of the Neder Rijn, Cpl. Smith and five men of his section were left behind as his boat was overloaded. He immediately searched and found another boat and took his men across. After several encounters with the enemy, being unable to find the rest of his company, he took up a defensive position at dawn which he held till the following night when he received orders to withdraw. He again searched and found an abandoned boat in which he brought his party back. Two nights later he volunteered to cross the river in company with an officer to search for stragglers. Throughout the entire operation Cpl. Smith showed exceptional coolness and powers of leadership."

'On the 25th September, 1944, during the assault on the Neder Rijn, Pte. Driver's Company Commander was seriously wounded in the legs after landing on the enemy shore. Pte. Driver, who was the Company Commander's batman, carried the officer to the river, found an assault boat and assisted him back across the river and as far as the R.A.P. This was done over 600 yards of river and ground, which was under continual mortar and small

[34] Eisenhower

arms fire. By his initiative and courage he undoubtedly saved the officer's life'[35].

The Times said of the operation: 'This story, which will rank with the great "relief" stories of British Army history, is of men who, with their own supply line cut behind them, drove ten miles through enemy-held fenland—with Tiger tanks crashing into the flying column—to get supplies through.' The difficulties in the way of mounting and maintaining the operation were indeed indescribable; the supply route through Holland was cut several times, and it was later revealed that the main road, indeed the only road, was open only for twelve hours during the entire operation[36]. Lieut.-Gen. Sir Frederick Browning, Deputy Commander of the Allied Airborne Army, later commented on the magnificent work done by the 4th Dorsets in the operation[37], which cost it thirteen officers and two hundred men[38].

---

[35]Citations [36]Hartwell [37]Wood [38]Unidentified Report

V

ON THE DEFENSIVE

AFTER Arnhem, the Battalion was generally in action, but in a defensive role that was destined to last many months[1]. It recrossed the Waal on the 4th October and went into divisional reserve at Heiligrand, just South-East of Nijmegen. 'We soon realised why this place was called the Holy Land, for all round us were various models, such as Calvary and Jerusalem. I went into a model church where everything was just as we were told about the Holy Land when we were children at school ... In our new positions everyone was accommodated under cover, but the local inhabitants did not like the idea of us occupying their Holy Land. ... To us of course, perhaps ignorant fellows, it was war on the Western Front, and we told them we were sorry'[2].

On the 8th the new C.O., Lieut.-Colonel W. Q. Roberts, arrived, and on the night of the 10th/11th the Battalion went into the line about two miles South of Groesbeek, itself some five miles South-East of Nijmegen. It was destined to remain in this area, though not always in the same locations, for exactly a month, and for most of the time was facing the Germans in the Reichswald Forest, just over the Dutch-German frontier less than two miles away.

On the 27th October a small party of the enemy put in an attack which failed completely, but the period was chiefly one of intensive patrolling by our own troops[3], and artillery duels. 'Our artillery laid on its usual fire plan, which meant that when Jerry fired five shells we replied with twenty-five to show him who were masters of the business'[4]. The following citation gives an idea of the way in which the month was spent: 'A fighting

[1]Roberts [2]Caines [3]Roberts [4]Caines

patrol was ordered forward of our positions to attack the enemy in a village street. The patrol penetrated the enemy positions and found itself in the centre of what was probably a company location. The patrol commander and second-in-command were both wounded, yet despite this, the private soldier took command, personally killed at least three Germans and eventually withdrew his patrol with only one man missing.' This soldier, Pte. P. A. Hyans, was awarded the Military Medal, and this is only one example of many valiant acts during those days[5]. The month from the 10th October to the 10th November was the least spectacular and the least eventful that the Battalion had yet spent, but it had reason to be pleased with itself, for it managed to subdue a numerically strong but morally weak enemy[6].

The month included one or two short periods of resting behind the lines, during which the Battalion was billeted in Dutch civilian houses; the owners were 'very willing and helpful; they offered their rooms, barns and farm buildings to accommodate us, sacrificing their own personal comfort, meaning that many families were bundled together in one room. . . . I was billeted in a very nice Dutch house, and found the occupants extremely helpful, my dirty underwear was quickly grabbed by a lady who insisted on washing it for me. They gave me milk and eggs and lit a fire in my room daily, and allowed me free use of the furniture'[7].

During one of these periods a visit was paid by the Corps Commander, who congratulated the Division on its fine performance in Holland and told it to busy itself preparing for the invasion of Germany.

In parts of the front the Allied Armies were already on German soil. On the 11th September the American First Army had entered the area of Trier, and on the 12th that of Aachen, though this first large German city to fall to the Allies was not finally cleared of the enemy until the 21st October[8]. But no serious attempt to invade Germany was possible until the port of Antwerp was opened, so that it was not until the middle of

[5]Roberts [6]Ibid [7]Caines [8]Eisenhower

November that the Northern and Central Groups of Armies could undertake an advance to the Rhine, which must be held from its mouth to Düsseldorf at least before a large-scale penetration beyond the river into Germany could be attempted[9].

The Eastward drive of the British-Canadian 21st Army Group, which began on the 15th November[10], included clearing the enemy salient West of the River Roer, sometimes called the Sittard Triangle. The enemy had been on the defensive for some weeks in this area, and had strengthened his position by digging, wiring, laying mines and constructing concrete pillboxes to the extent of making it an outpost of the Siegfried Line. The British 30th Corps, of which the 43rd Division was part, was placed under command of the American Ninth Army for this operation, the task of the Division being to protect the American left flank and to open the Sittard-Geilenkirchen road for supplies[11]. The part that the 4th Dorsets were to play in this operation, the first real attack on German soil, was the capture of the village of Straeten, about four miles North of Geilenkirchen[12].

The Battalion left the Nijmegen-Groesbeek area at 0930 hrs on the 11th November, travelled South 120 miles without incident, and at 2145 hrs reached the village of Groetdoenrade, three miles South-East of Sittard. It found the Triangle a hive of activity. 'Every day more and more tanks seemed to appear in the area, amongst them were flame-throwers and flail tanks used for mine clearing'[13].

If the month spent in the Nijmegen-Groesbeek area had been its most uneventful, that spent in the Sittard Triangle was to be its most frustrating; the rest of the Division, indeed the rest of the Brigade, were able to cover themselves with glory, but every time the 4th Dorsets were ordered to go into action the orders were cancelled before the moment for action arrived.

The Battalion was first ordered to capture Straeten, on the 19th, and in the morning actually formed up in its assembly area, but the attack was postponed twice, and eventually on the night of the 20th the Battalion went to relieve the 5th Dorsets in the

[9]Eisenhower [10]Ibid [11]Hartwell [12]Matthews [13]Caines

wood West of Tripsrath[14], later known as 'Dorset Wood', which the 5th Dorsets, with D Company of the 4th Dorsets under command[15], had captured in the morning, after capturing Bauchem by a brilliant operation on the 18th[16]. Apart from odd incursions during raids in the previous month, this relief brought the 4th Dorsets onto German soil for the first time.

Major Matthews, who was commanding D Company, has written the following account of the attack and the subsequent relief:

'On the 18th November the 5th Dorsets captured Bauchem, a suburb of Geilenkirchen, and the 1st Worcesters took Tripsrath. The latter were in difficulties as the enemy had taken up positions in the woods surrounding the village and were counter-attacking in force. As the Northern edge of the woods to the West of Tripsrath was to be the startline for another attack, it was essential that the area should be cleared.

'Next day the 5th Dorsets, with a squadron of the 13/18th Hussars in support, attacked the woods. The leading companies came under heavy fire, which caused casualties and held up their advance. The exposed forward companies were able to move to cover, but further movement in the woods was impracticable that night.

'The 4th Dorsets had meanwhile dug in in the woods South of Gangelt, and awaited the successful completion of the 5th Dorsets' attack before launching their own on Straeten.

'During the night a new plan was made, and the Brigade Commander ordered the 4th Dorsets to provide a company to support the 5th in a fresh attack. At 0010 hrs on the 20th my company received orders to join the 5th Dorsets, and we moved up in darkness in the early hours of the morning. I had barely received my orders before the vigorous attack went in at daybreak supported by artillery, and initially by tanks. This attack was entirely successful, and by 1000 hrs D Company of the 5th had reached its objective, which was the northernmost edge of the woods. A and C Companies, amalgamated owing to

[14]W.D. [15]Matthews [16]Hartwell

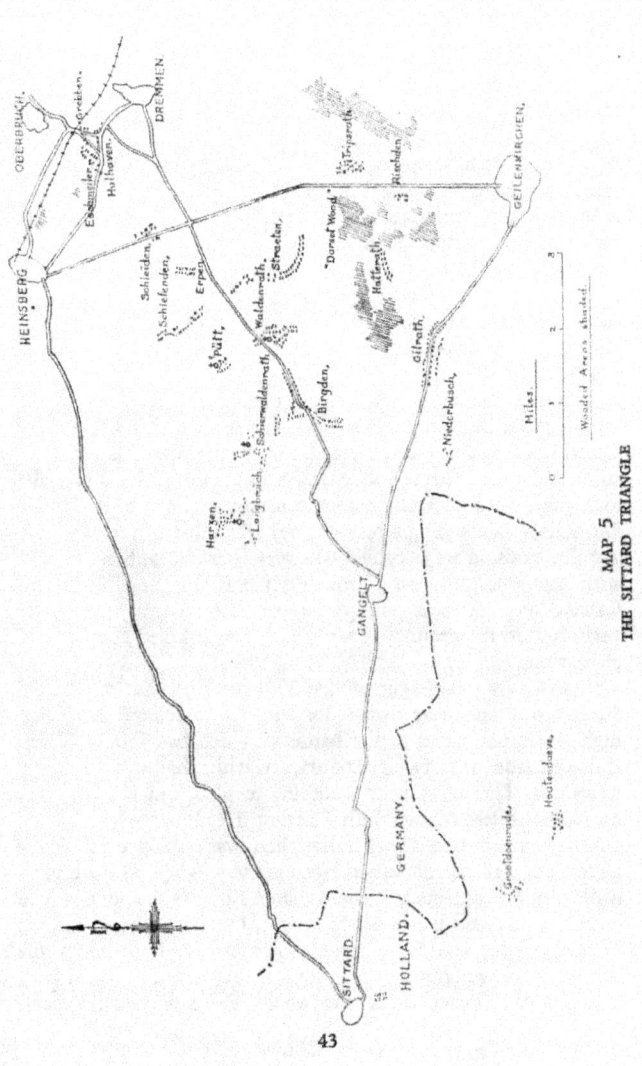

MAP 5
THE SITTARD TRIANGLE

heavy casualties, shortly afterwards reached the top of the wood overlooking Tripsrath. My company, which was in immediate support, followed A and C Companies and took a few prisoners in the process of mopping up. The tanks were unable to give the infantry much support as the going was very muddy, and only one troop managed to get forward. The enemy reacted violently, and during the advance my company was subjected to heavy shelling from S.P. guns and mortars and suffered a number of casualties. The enemy tried several times to form up for a counter-attack, but the quick co-operation of our artillery was responsible for dispersing them before they were able to launch an attack.

'We then dug in in the woods behind D Company of the 5th Dorsets, but after a few hours we were ordered to relieve A and C Companies in the North arm of the wood, as the latter companies were reduced in strength to about forty. The relief took place with difficulty under constant shelling, and Captain Dominie, commanding a platoon, was killed during the move up.

"The position we occupied was very isolated, with no contact with the other forward company. It was not possible to get forward any anti-tank guns to support the company. We were very thin on the ground, as we had lost four killed and twenty-eight wounded.

'Shortly after midnight on the 20th the Brigadier visited the 5th Dorsets and gave orders for the 4th to relieve them that night—welcome news to the battalion which had fought a continuous battle for forty-eight hours, and which had suffered heavy casualties. The relief went according to plan, but my company had lost wireless contact with Battalion Headquarters and could not be warned that the 4th Battalion was taking over. Some alarm was felt at Battalion Headquarters when D Company could not be contacted. Lieut.-Colonel Roberts sent out several patrols to try and locate us that night, but it was several hours before contact could be made. For twenty-four hours the company was without food or water.

'The 4th Dorsets held the woods for nearly eight days.

Patrolling was carried out at night, and some minefields were laid in front of the forward positions.'

The 21st was spent digging in and pumping water out of the flooded trenches to the accompaniment of a continuous downpour of shells[17]. On the 22nd 'weasels' were allotted to bring up rations and essential supplies, but the meals invariably arrived cold owing to hours being needed to bring them through the mud. This could be done only during the hours of darkness, which entailed an evening meal at midnight and breakfast at 4.0 a.m.[18]. The Battalion Quartermaster, Captain H. A. S. Titterington, 'whose unsparing efforts contributed very largely to the high morale of the Battalion,' was awarded the M.B.E. for the magnificent work he did during the week[19]. Many men were ill with influenza, trench feet or sheer exhaustion, and the only drop of comfort was the rum that was issued twice daily[20]. On the 26th the 5th Wilts were ordered to clear the Northern tip of Tripsrath[21], but the enemy must have thought that the attack was coming from the 4th Dorsets' area, for the Battalion 'received its heaviest shelling ever'[22]. Shelling and mortaring, indeed, had been continuous throughout the week; the forward companies suffered heavily, and D Company lost half its effective strength in four days.

Colonel Roberts has written the following account of the operation:

'For continuous discomfort, for every reason, the holding of "Dorset Wood" by the 4th Dorsets was both remarkable and an achievement of which the Battalion can justly be proud. It has been said frequently that the British soldier is at his best when up against real adversity and this was a typical instance. From the part played by D Company, under Major Guy Matthews, which was attached to the 5th Dorsets for an attack on the wood, until the Fourth Battalion was finally relieved by the 1st Worcesters, after a whole week in the line, the courage and fortitude displayed by all ranks was of the highest order.

'The Battalion relieved the 5th Dorsets immediately after this

[17]Caines [18]Matthews [19]Citation [20]Caines [21]W.D. [22]Caines

attack and took over partly prepared positions which, although not under direct observation, were well known to the enemy who had previously been in occupation. The shell and mortar fire was both sustained and accurate throughout the week, causing many casualties, although discipline with regard to movement was rigorously controlled and enforced. The situation was particularly aggravated by the fact that weather conditions were little short of appalling. The area was a sea of mud and consequently all slit trenches were water-logged and required frequent baling. No transport other than "weasels" could move, and our own transport, together with the Tank Squadron of the 13th/18th Hussars, was completely bogged down. First class recovery work was subsequently carried out by the Divisional R.E.M.E. under heavy fire, and the C.R.E.M.E., Lieut.-Colonel Neilson, personally supervised much of this difficult operation.

'Everyone appreciated the necessity of maintaining morale and of making the best of an unpleasant situation. Brigadier B. A. Coad came up daily and was thoughtful enough to bring me some shaving water, as that very essential commodity was in short supply. This was duly shared out, and Company Commanders visited Battalion Headquarters for shaving parties—an innovation —as there was rarely enough water for them after their companies had been "watered and shaved". The Battery Commander, Major Peter Steele-Perkins, did valiant work in supporting the Battalion upon every possible occasion. We had a rule that in any gun duel the last salvo would be fired by the Royal Artillery of the 43rd Division. This rule was faithfully adhered to and our gunners often fired late into the early hours of the morning. The Battalion Signallers, Snipers and Intelligence Section did a first class job of work maintaining communications and often coming in with valuable information as to enemy positions on our front, line parties, snipers and Intelligence personnel frequently having been subjected to heavy shell, mortar and small arms fire during the course of their duties.

'The daily visit to companies took some two hours at least, and the I.O., Lieut. John Adams, and I used to congratulate each other when we got back, but we were inspired throughout by the spirit of the men, whose dogged example was sufficient to make us swallow our own fears when we found them often standing in water, plastered in mud, but still smiling.

'The Quartermaster, Captain Titterington, as usual did his very best under these somewhat exceptional conditions. The cooks were established close to the Battalion in a separate detachment of A Echelon in a position where their safety was a matter of conjecture, but from where there was just a little hope of the meals not being entirely cold by the time the "weasels" had ploughed a sticky course to the company R.V. for carrying parties. It was inevitable that these carrying parties suffered casualties and that others were hit during the course of issuing ammunition, meals and water.

'The position was finally handed over to the 1st Worcesters after a week of unmitigated discomfort. Curiously enough, not a shot was fired during the relief and we marched out in good order for a short period of rest and for a much needed opportunity of refitting and maintenance. There was nothing spectacular about that week, but the men of Dorset just stuck it out and stuck it out damned well.'

The relief on the night of the 28th was a relief indeed, and the Battalion moved back to Shinveld, about eight miles away from the shooting[23], where it got much needed baths and clean clothes[24].

On the 30th November the Battalion relieved the 4th Wilts in Trispsrath, where it spent four days patrolling; on the 5th December it withdrew to Geilenkirchen, and on the 7th to Hoensbroek in Holland, about half way between Geilenkirchen and Maastricht. The Division was preparing for a large-scale operation, in conjunction with the Americans, to cut off the enemy salient West of the River Roer[25], in which the task of the 4th Dorsets was to attack in the area Tripsrath-Hatterath; the attack was timed to begin on the 12th, but bad weather

[23]W.D. [24]Caines [25]Hartwell

caused continual postponements[26], and the Battalion was again cheated of its chance of offensive action.

On the 17th the Battalion was ordered to withdraw to the Tilburg area[27], for some weeks of intensive training[28], and the advance party actually left, but on the 16th General Field-Marshal von Rundstedt started the counter-offensive in the Ardennes ordered by Hitler, with the object of seizing first the key maintenance and communications centre of Liège and then the great supply port of Antwerp[29]. Potentially this German drive was appallingly dangerous, and formations, of which the 43rd Division was one, had to be moved South to meet it.

The 4th Dorsets left Hoensbroek on the morning of the 19th and arrived at Hasselt, in Eastern Belgium, the same evening. 'The people there were friendly and could not do enough for us, but I also found them upset and shivering with fear because they believed it was possible for Jerry to return; apparently they had heard the six o'clock news when it was reported that Jerry was still pushing on, and the Americans were still unable to check the advance. Yes, it was certainly a sad story, but we were not worried, we all had great confidence in Montgomery'[30]. While the Battalion was at Hasselt the ballot was held for the first seven days' leave in England.

On the 23rd the Battalion moved to the area of Waremme-Hollogne-sur-Geer, about twelve miles North of the Meuse at Huy. 'As we passed through the Belgian villages and towns the inhabitants cheered us by, we never quite knew why, but presumed because it was the presence of British troops again'[31]. Christmas was spent here in bitterly cold weather; morning tea was taken to all the men by the officers and sergeants, who also waited on them in the mess, where the Quartermaster managed to serve an excellent dinner[32]. As no orders to move had been received by the 26th, the Battalion gave a Boxing Day dance in the village hall at Grande Axe[33].

[26]Hartwell [27]W.D. [28]Hartwell [29]Eisenhower [30]Caines [31]Ibid [32]Ibid. Sergt. Caines was commissioned on the 19th December after having commanded the Signals Platoon for many weeks without an officer. [33]Ibid.

The few days spent in Central Belgium were by no means all given up to pleasure; the Battalion had moved there to help to stem the German push, and on Christmas afternoon the C.O. and the Company Commanders reconnoitred a defensive position in the hills South of Huy. It never had to be used, for by the 26th the enemy offensive was halted within four miles of the Meuse[34], but it was still considered possible for von Rundstedt to make a thrust in the British sector further North[35], and the 43rd Division moved back to the Sittard Triangle. On the 27th the 4th Dorsets moved to Groot Haasdal, in the extreme South of Holland, about fifteen miles North-West of Aachen. The men were billeted on the inhabitants, who did not seem to welcome them with much pleasure, but who got friendly later[36]. While in this area, where it remained for seventeen days, the Battalion had the task of digging alternative defensive positions at Kolleberg, immediately South of Sittard, and at Alsdorf, about twelve miles North-East of Aachen. This was hard work, as snow began to fall heavily on the 28th, and froze solidly on the 30th[37]; in fact the ground was so hard that much of the 'digging in' had to be done by blasting the soil with Hawkins grenades[38]. In the event, neither position was ever occupied by the Battalion, for the German offensive had spent its force more than was at first realised, and the threat to the British sector, if it ever existed, never materialised.

The Battalion was still at Groot Haasdal at the end of the year, and on the 31st December it held a New Year's party and nearly everyone stayed up to see the New Year in[39]. It was no ordinary year that was dawning, for 1945 was to see the total collapse of the 'Wehrmacht' and the end of the war in Europe, and by the 1st January more than half the Battalion's work had been done.

---

[34]Eisenhower [35]Caines [36]Ibid [37]Ibid [38]Symonds [39]Caines

VI

THE INVASION OF GERMANY

By the 16th January 1945 the Battle of the Ardennes was substantially concluded, and the Allied line was again able to take up the order in which it had been ranged along the threshold of Germany at the time of von Rundstedt's offensive a month earlier. The immediate purpose of the Allies was now to eliminate all the enemy remaining West of the Rhine in order to reduce to a minimum the number of forces that would otherwise be available to oppose the crossing of that immense water barrier[1].

In early January the 43rd Division returned to complete the task which it had begun in November, but which had been held up by bad weather and interrupted by the Ardennes offensive—the clearing of the Sittard Triangle, and on the 12th the 4th Dorsets, amidst snow and ice[2], relieved the 5th K.O.S.B. in the Niederbusch area, about four miles West of Geilenkirchen. The 130th Brigade was allotted a counter-attack rôle in the earlier part of the operation[3], and took up a second-line position behind the 129th Brigade[4]. 'Jerry on the whole was very quiet, but occasionally a shower of shells would come over and bursts from machine guns would be heard in the distance'[5].

On the 21st, when there was a foot of snow on the ground[6], the Battalion as a whole took the offensive for the first time since Arnhem and attacked Schierwaldenrath, about three miles due North of Niederbusch, A and C Companies leading. As strong opposition was expected, the preparations for this attack were very thorough, even including flying the company commanders over the objective the day before. Vehicles and equipment were

[1]Eisenhower [2]Caines [3]Hartwell [4]Caines [5]Ibid [6]Symonds

whitewashed, snow suits issued to many of the men, and Sherman tanks draped in white sheets[7].

The village was protected by mines and booby traps, which delayed the advance, but enemy shelling, which was particularly heavy as the village was entered[8], was the only effective opposition. The attack started at 0830 hrs[9]; by 1500 hrs the objective was completely cleared, and fourteen prisoners had been taken for the cost of two casualties[10]. It was not possible to hoist the Union Jack over the village until the 24th, as it had to be washed first[11]. On the same afternoon the 5th Dorsets captured Harzeltlangbroich[12], to the Battalion's left, and the 7th Hampshires Putt and Waldenrath[13] to its right. The Battalion suffered some casualties from enemy shelling during the night[14], during which patrols were sent out to clear possible mines on the road to Pütt[15]; they returned with a large number of prisoners[16].

On the 22nd, 'Jerry had cooled off and started to pull back to Heinsberg,' and the news was received that the 7th Armoured Division had reached Roermond[17], at the junction of the Roer and the Meuse. On the 24th the 4th Dorsets were ordered to capture Eschweiler and Grebben, two miles South-East of Heinsberg, and at 1300 hrs on the 25th the operation known as 'Jug II' began[18], in extremely cold and frosty weather[19], with A Company leading. By 1700 hrs the objective was gained; no opposition was encountered[20] and artillery support was not even necessary, as the enemy had pulled out before the attack started[21]. Nevertheless, there were a few stragglers, and nine prisoners were taken. The village was undamaged, but only a few stragglers remained; 'we found them scared stiff, for fear of what we might do to them'[22]; they were allowed to remain in their houses.

There was some slight enemy shelling and mortaring during the night, and on the 26th a patrol from A Company, under Major Symonds, went to Oberbruch, three miles further on, and found it deserted by its inhabitants. However, the enemy still had out-

[7]Symonds [8]Caines [9]Symonds [10]Ibid [11]Ibid [12]Hartwell [13]Caines [14]Ibid [15]W.D. [16]Caines [17]Ibid [18]W.D. [19]Caines [20]W.D. [21]Caines [22]Ibid

posts there, for this patrol suffered a few casualties in contact with one of them, and those sent out during the next three days met with opposition[23].

The Sittard Triangle was eliminated by the 31st January[24], and after these actions, in which the Battalion had had to do little more than show the flag, the 43rd Division was withdrawn from the line and sent to Northern Belgium[25], to prepare for the major assault that was being planned on the Siegfried Line[26]. The Battalion left the Heinsberg area on the 29th, and moved by easy stages to Turnhout, about twenty-five miles East of Antwerp, where it arrived on the 3rd February. A thaw had set in on the 1st, and the weather was mild, but very damp, and all the roads were a sea of mud[27]. At Turnhout the Battalion was billeted very comfortably; the Belgians gave up all the accommodation they could to fit it in, and were generally most helpful[28].

Before an assault crossing of the Rhine could be undertaken, there were still considerable enemy forces to be eliminated between that river and the Meuse, and in order to deal with them, Operation 'Veritable' was planned with the object of destroying all the enemy West of the Rhine from the Nijmegen bridgehead as far South as the general line Jülich-Düsseldorf[29].

The enemy defences in the area were organised in three main zones: West of the Reichswald Forest there was a belt of defences two thousand yards deep; about three kilometres East of this forward position was the northern end of the Siegfried Line, whose main belt ran from the Cleve-Nijmegen road over the high ground in the Reichswald to the heavily defended town of Goch, whence it continued to Geldern, and thence along a slight lip which overlooked the valley of the Meuse as far as Roermond; about ten kilometres to the East again was the defensive system known as the 'lay-back', which ran from the Rhine opposite Rees to Geldern, and then on to the South[30].

Gigantic preparations were made for this operation, in which the whole offensive strength of the 21st Army Group was to be

[23]Symonds [24]Hartwell [25]W.D. [26]Hartwell [27]Caines [28]Ibid [29]Field-Marshal Montgomery: 'Normandy to the Baltic' [30]Ibid

employed, and for which the American Ninth Army was to be placed under British operational command[31].

The Canadian First Army, with the British 30th Corps under command, was to launch a strong offensive South-Eastwards from the Nijmegen area, break through the Reichswald Forest, and clear the land between the Meuse and the Rhine to the general line Xanten-Geldern[32]. The attack, which was to be launched by the 30th Corps, was planned on a one-corps front, with the Canadian 2nd, and the British 15th, 51st and 53rd Divisions leading[33]. The 43rd Division was to concentrate in the Nijmegen area, and from there push through the Reichswald Forest to South of Goch, and so roll up the Siegfried Line 'lay-back'; this was to be done by a series of battalion attacks, one passing through the other[34]. Extensive preliminary air operations were undertaken against railway bridges and ferries serving the enemy area, and, on the night preceding the assault, Bomber Command heavily raided Cleve, Goch and the main communications centres and billeting areas in the enemy's rear[35].

The 4th Dorsets left Turnhout on the 7th, travelled through Helmond and Eindhoven, and arrived at Nijmegen on the afternoon of the 9th. 'The town was packed with troops, and the attack having started, was frequently shelled. One shell landed on a gasometer; the top flew in the air and kept circling about overhead, but landed without hurting anybody.... Ambulances with wounded were continually bumping their way through shell holes'[36].

The attack had been opened by the 15th Scottish Division early on the morning of the 8th, and was known to be going well[37]. The 4th Dorsets were warned to be ready to move early on the 10th, but the advance was continually postponed, and they did not leave the Nijmegen area till 0115 hrs on the 13th. On that day the Battalion again entered German territory, and at 0600 hrs stopped on the Northern edge of the Reichswald, about two miles South of Cleve.

[31]Montgomery: *op. cit.* [32]Eisenhower [33]Montgomery: *op. cit.* [34]Hartwell [35]Montgomery: *op. cit.* [36]Caines [37]Ibid

Major Symonds has written the following account of the part played by the Battalion in Operation 'Veritable':

'We moved in T.C.V.'s from Nijmegen and took up defensive positions in the Reichswald Forest on the 13th. That evening we moved to Cleve and found that ancient town a mass of ruins. No house, building, or even tree was left intact. The roads were cratered everywhere, and dead German soldiers and civilians were numerous. We moved in after dark and the whole place seemed most weird.

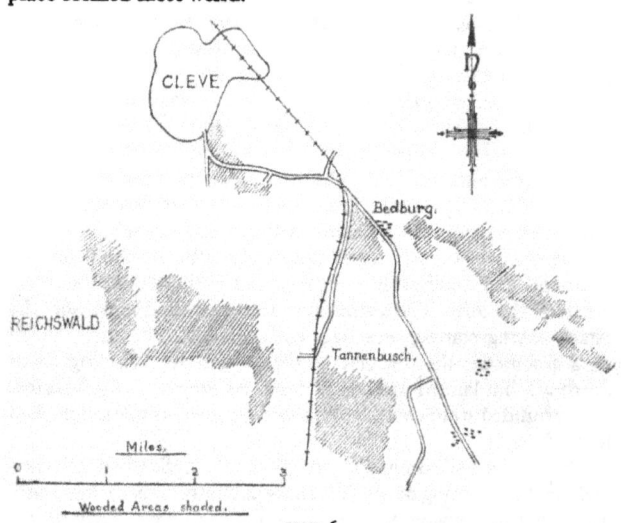

MAP 6
THE REICHSWALD

'We spent the night in cellars amongst Canadian troops, and moved off on the morning of the 14th to relieve the 5th Wilts about a mile South of Bedburg, some three miles to the East. The Wilts were preparing to attack Southwards themselves and were being counter-attacked at the time also. However, the relief took place without serious incident, for by this stage of the war we were getting pretty experienced at these matters. We held the position throughout the 14th without incident other than shelling.

'During the night we were called to Battalion Headquarters for orders to attack through the 5th Wilts in the morning. We hung about there for a long time, waiting for Lieut.-Colonel Roberts to return from Brigade. When he returned he gave us orders to pass through the 5th Wilts and capture several hamlets quite deep in enemy territory. The Germans were fighting very hard here, and we were opposed by a battalion from a parachute regiment. We were to attack with A Company (now my company) leading on the left and C Company (under Major Robert Gill) on the right. B and D Companies were to pass through us when we reached our objectives.

As we approached the start line we discovered that it was not secured, the 5th Wilts not in fact being as far advanced as was reported, so we had to hurriedly select another start line several hundred yards to the rear. We were supported by a squadron of Sherman tanks, but these were not as much help as they might have been, as they could not get along properly owing to the wet state of the ground.

'Whilst I was "recce-ing" the start line with the other company commanders we noticed German air burst shells registering overhead, and my batman, Pte. Danniels, suggested that we meet the company and form them up a little to the left and rear of the newly chosen place, where there was a German trench system. This I did, very fortunately, as when the company arrived we were treated to a most tremendous shelling which could only have been the result of observed fire. The enemy was in fact still in strong occupation of some high ground and houses which we had understood were clear. I had never, before or since, been the object of such concentrated shelling as attended us whilst we were trying to form up for this attack. The result was that we were about ten minutes late in getting under way, which we did at 1000 hrs.

'No. 2 Platoon, under Lieut. Girardot, was leading my company, and came under heavy small arms fire from the houses and gardens on the high ground to our front before we had gone far, and was pinned to the ground, Lieut. Girardot being wounded and Sgt. Gregory killed. After locating the enemy positions with some difficulty I launched an attack with No. 1 Platoon under command of Lieut. Pope. No. 3 Platoon had got somewhat broken up by the enemy defensive fire and could not be got into this attack, so the remaining members supported No. 1 Platoon's assault with two-inch mortar smoke and small arms fire.

'My F.O.O. fired a concentration on the objective but, although it was accurate, it was not as heavy as he was usually able to produce owing to shortage of ammunition caused by the flooded lines of communication.

'No. 1 Platoon assaulted with splendid courage but was badly shot up on approaching the enemy positions by the German paratroopers, who were dug in in the cellars of the houses and were firing from ground level, and had consequently not been much battered by our twenty-five pounders' concentration.

'By this time we had been able to get a troop of Shermans up, which had previously been unable to get along with us owing to the wet state of the ground, so I launched another assault on the enemy positions with the available members of No. 3 Platoon and such remaining members of Nos. 1 and 2 as it was possible to gather up. This assault, supported by three Shermans, went well, and the Germans ran out of the rear of the houses as we rushed in through the front gardens. We were able to shoot down a good many of them as they withdrew across the open fields beyond.

' C Company on our right met equally stiff opposition and had to fight very hard to capture the houses on the high ground to their immediate front also. Although neither A nor C Companies had yet reached their allotted objectives, they did in fact overcome the enemy and capture his principal positions, and the remainder of the Germans withdrew.

'As both my officers were badly wounded and my company

much depleted, I consolidated on the captured ground at about 1220 hrs, as did C Company for similar reasons.

'From the approach of the Battalion to the F.U.P. until the Germans had been dislodged from the houses on the high ground, they treated us to almost continuous shelling and mortaring, at times so heavy that it was virtually impossible to count the shells falling, all of which made the attack very difficult; however, the men behaved magnificently throughout and there were many cases of exceptional calmness and bravery among them.'

Colonel Roberts has added the following:

'The 15th February, 1945, was, in my opinion, the toughest day experienced by the 4th Dorsets during my period of command. The whole of "F" Echelon of the Battalion was subjected to both continuous shell and mortar fire from the time that the original start line was reached until nightfall. It was estimated that the enemy had well over 300 guns in support of this sector, and we seemed to be the target of most of them!

'I had misgivings as to whether the leading companies would leave the start line in good order, but at H-Hour C Company on the right and A Company on the left, ably led by Majors Robert Gill and Joe Symonds respectively, were well deployed and advanced towards their initial objectives disregarding the very heavy fire which was directed upon them by the enemy. In fact I was amazed that the advance continued in the early stages as steadily as it did. I shall always carry a vivid picture of the tall figure of Major Symonds standing up, blowing his whistle, and bowling his steel helmet in the direction of the Germans. A Company appreciated this typical gesture by its commander and followed him to a man. At the same time a very large piece of shrapnel struck a wall in the gap of about a foot that separated the I.O., Lieut. John Adams and the Mortar Officer, Captain Gordon Perring. The look of surprise on their faces, no doubt caused by the fact that they still lived, was encouraging to a degree, more particularly as, in the next minute, a mortar bomb burst just short of the Battery Commander's scout-car, where we were arranging another "Canadian Mattress" for the benefit of the Forest of Cleve on our exposed right flank.

A and C Companies soon met some very tough opposition fom German paratroops forming part of Battle Group Hutze—the officer who had succeeded van der Heidte, after his capture during the Ardennes offensive. A Company finally took its objective, a set of farm buildings at the top of a commanding feature, which reminded one of the main objective on a cloth model exercise, after no less than three attempts. With grim and unrelenting determination it finally took that hill, giving no quarter and pursuing and killing more of the enemy, who decided to run. Returning in a tank from this pursuit, Major Symonds was seriously burnt when the tank received a direct hit from an 88 mm. gun and "brewed up" at once. With his usual thoroughness, however, he reorganised the remnants of his company and was finally evacuated in great pain. I did not expect to see him again before the end of the war, but of course he returned to the Battalion and to A Company in a month's time, having flatly refused to be sent home to England.

'On the right C Company had an equally prolonged scrap at close quarters amongst farm buildings and cottages. In the first few minutes after making contact the officers threw away the carbines they had acquired from our gallant allies and picked up S.M.L.E. rifles from their own casualties, as they found them to be more effective! Major Gill was soon wounded and the Company finally captured its objective under the equally brave leadership of the second-in-command, Captain John Kirkwood.

' B Company, under Major Mike Whittle, was subsequently passed through to the end of the spur immediately to our front, and occupied a position some thousand yards beyond A and C Companies. I spent an interesting time with the I.O. finding them in the dark with the aid of a compass and a good deal of luck. In the course of our wanderings we heard much German conversation, but I think that most were civilians!

'That night, Brigadier Aubrey Coad visited Battalion Headquarters, in what was left of a farmhouse, as a mark of his esteem, and left us a very large and good looking bottle with a most fascinating label, that promised nectar to a very tired team of officers, Signallers, Intelligence personnel and snipers. The Adjutant, Captain Tony Cottle, found glasses in the cellar and in some solemnity we were about to toast the Regiment, when we discovered that the bottle contained malt vinegar! The customary visit of the Quartermaster, Captain Sam Titterington, who always came up with unfailing regularity, was even more welcome when he produced a rum issue!'

As a result of this operation Major Symonds was awarded a Bar to his Military Cross. He 'displayed superb gallantry throughout. He was everywhere about the battlefield inspiring his men by his own total disregard for his personal safety'[38].

At nightfall the Battalion was ordered to stand fast, and the 7th Hampshires and 5th Dorsets to pass through[39]; the enemy had evidently not retreated very far, for the area was shelled and mortared all night. An enemy patrol unsuccessfully attacked B Company at 0120 hrs on the 16th, and at 0445 hrs a patrol of D Company took twelve prisoners.

On the 16th, the 214th Brigade attacked Goch. The attack was a great success and hundreds of prisoners were taken[40]. The town itself was captured on the 19th by the 15th Scottish Division[41]. The 4th Dorsets stayed in their positions throughout the 16th[42], and were shelled all that night[43]. At 1000 hrs on the 17th they began to attack the Tannenbusch, a wood about a mile square half a mile to the West; no opposition was encountered, the wood was reported clear of the enemy by all four companies by 1330 hrs, and at 1430 hrs the Battalion returned to its previous day's positions.

On the afternoon of the 18th the Battalion was relieved and returned to Cleve, which had been blasted to pieces by the R.A.F. to the extent that there was literally not one building standing[44]. For the next three weeks it was to guard the South bank of the Rhine in locations varying from Warbeyen, opposite Emmerich, to Millingen, at the point where the Rhine divides

[38]Citation [39]Caines [40]Ibid [41]Ibid [42]W.D. [43]Caines [44]Ibid

to become the Waal and the Lek, its main task being to watch the enemy on the North bank. Two companies were to be in the line at a time[45], and the remainder of the Battalion was to remain at Cleve[46].

Heavy rain began to fall on the 19th; the roads were again a sea of mud and the whole area North of Cleve to the river, a distance of roughly four miles, was under water[47], the floods in places being four feet deep[48]. However, waterproof equipment, including rubber dinghies, and food and water for several days were issued[49], and at 1500 hrs on the 20th the two forward companies embarked in buffaloes and got into position by 2330 hrs. 'The journey was an extremley funny experience, as all one could see for miles around were the tops of trees and houses. The floods began to go down rapidly, and the personnel was reasonably housed in comparatively good billets, mostly on the second floor'[50]. On the 23rd the floods had subsided enough for the Carrier Platoon to be established in the area of Warbeyen, to block any possible enemy infiltration from the East.

On the 12th, the Battalion moved back to the area Bergen-Aalen-Langstraat, on the East bank of the Maas, about eight miles South-East of Goch[51], to do some final training for the crossing of the Rhine, which was to take place in a few days[52]. The sun had begun to shine on the 8th, the roads had turned to dust, and the weather had become very warm indeed[53]. While in this area, information was received from a reliable source that hundreds of bottles of wine were buried near Cleve. Captain Richards took a party to look for them, and after hours of digging returned with 1,600 bottles of cognac. Many parties were held, and a mobile reserve was formed which followed the Battalion from place to place[54].

The crossing of the Rhine began on the night of the 23rd/24th March. The initial assault in the British 30th Corps area was made by the 51st Highland Division[55]. The 43rd Division was given the task of following up the assault and breaking out of the

[45]W.D. [46]Caines [47]Ibid [48]W.D. [49]Caines [50]Ibid [51]W.D. [52]Caines [53]Ibid [54]Ibid [55]Eisenhower

bridgehead; it was to capture Anholt, Dinxperlo and Aalten, and to open the way for the Guards Armoured Division, whose advance was to have no limit[56].

The 4th Dorsets reached their marshalling area, Marienbaum, some four miles North-West of Xanten, at 1400 hrs on the 24th[57] after a blinding journey along dusty roads, under a sky that was black with aircraft and gliders[58]. By this time the 51st Division was across; it had fought bitterly and had been counter-attacked several times by fanatical enemy paratroops[59], but by 1700 hrs its bridgehead, in the area of Rees, measured some three miles by one and a half. The Battalion spent the night, luckily a warm one, and the following day in the fields, and at 2030 hrs on the 25th left for its point of embarkation, where it arrived at 0030 hrs on the 26th[60], after a terribly slow journey through the gun area[61].

At 0100 hrs on the 26th the crossing began in buffaloes with no enemy interference, and by 0200 hrs the whole Battalion was across one mile West of Rees, and Battalion Headquarters were established at Esserden. 'The area was shelled frequently, but on the whole we found it much quieter than we expected, and therefore the odd shell did not bother us a great deal'[62].

The 5th Dorsets had crossed on the afternoon of the 25th and had occupied the village of Speldrop, but were unable to capture Androp as the open country was under observation from the high ground beyond the long, narrow lake known as the Millingenmeer[63]. On the 26th the 4th Dorsets passed through the Canadian Brigade, which was held up on the left, and attacked the village of Millingen[64]. A few minutes before the assault began, Typhoons came and fired rockets into the village and at the same time 25-pounders plastered the place with shells and smoke[65]. The attack began at 1515 hrs; A Company, under Major Symonds, led, with the task of capturing a river bridge and the approaches to Millingen[66]; by 1810 hrs the leading company had established a bridgehead across the Millingenmeer, and at 1930 hrs D

[56]Hartwell [57]W.D. [58]Caines [59]Hartwell [60]W.D. [61]Caines [62]Ibid
[63]Hartwell [64]Roberts [65]Caines [66]Roberts

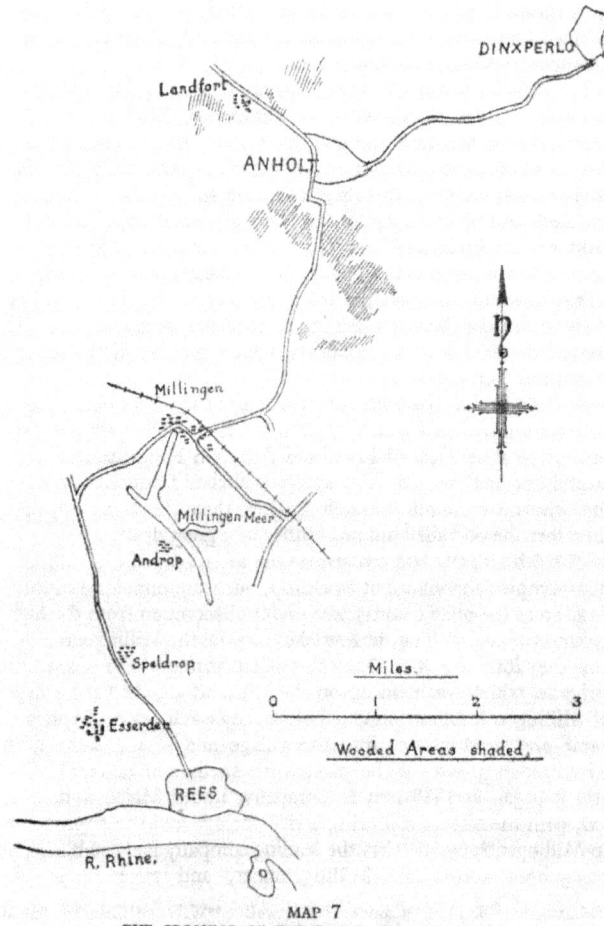

MAP 7
THE CROSSING OF THE RHINE AND MILLINGEN

Company passed through and extended the bridgehead to the right. At 2230 hrs B Company went through and cleared the ground to the railway, one mile South-East of Millingen, and by 0200 hrs on the 27th C Company consolidated the position in the village itself.

'The battle went entirely according to plan and by the early hours of the morning the 4th Dorsets had taken Millingen with some 190 prisoners of war, and with the loss of only a few casualties, and for the one and only time none were fatal. Sound junior leadership and a fair knowledge of street fighting technique by officers, N.C.O.'s and men were responsible for this success'[67]. There was stubborn fighting in some of the houses, and 'in many we found civilians packed into cellars; many at first were scared stiff of us, they just breathed a sigh of relief when we spoke to them and convinced them that they would come to no harm'[68].

Colonel Roberts received a Bar to his D.S.O. for his part in this operation, the success of which 'was due to his coolness and judgement under fire, and the example that he set to his company commanders enabled a most difficult operation to be carried through successfully with very few casualties'[69].

The capture of Millingen made possible the final stages of the 130th Brigade's task in the establishment of the bridgehead over the Rhine—the securing of the crossing over the Oude Ijssel at Landfort[70], about three miles to the North—and on the 27th the 5th Dorsets attacked it. After spending the night being heavily shelled at Millingen, the 4th Dorsets joined in the attack at 1430 hrs on the 28th, B Company leading. By 1800 hrs. B Company had secured the crossing over the canal immediately South of Landfort, and by 2230 hrs A Company, which had passed through, was firm on the South side of the Oude Ijssel, while by 2330 hrs C Company had mopped up the small wood immediately to the West and was also firm on the South bank of the river.

During the night of the 28th/29th, the 5th Dorsets enlarged

[67]Roberts [68]Caines [69]Citation [70]Hartwell

their bridgehead over the Oude Ijssel at Landfort[71], and at 0815 hrs on the 29th the 4th Dorsets passed through to capture Anholt. B Company, the leading company, only met with a little shelling and mortaring from the enemy, and by 1010 hrs had secured its first objective without difficulty. At 1015 hrs A and C Companies passed through and reported that the roads in the towns were blocked with trees, mines and road blocks, but they were firmly on their objectives by 1400 hrs, and D Company passed through them and consolidated in the centre of the battered town.

On the same day the 7th Hampshires, who had been on the left of the 4th Dorsets during the capture of Landfort, made a dash to the East and captured Dinxperlo[72], thereby completing the task allotted to the Brigade in the crossing of the Rhine and the establishment of a bridgehead on its right bank. The task of the Division was also ended, as the breakout from the bridgehead was now completed. Opposition had never been heavy, but demolitions were plentiful, and it had been necessary to maintain constant pressure ever since the crossing[73]. Germany had been successfully invaded, her great natural bastion lay behind the Battalion, and before it the road lay open to any part of the country to which it might be ordered to go.

---

[71]Caines [72]Hartwell [73]Ibid

VII

THE COLLAPSE

'Within a week of the crossing of the Rhine, the Allied spearheads were thrusting Eastwards, isolating corps and divisions, and cutting off one army from another. Despair gripped the German forces as never before, and the disintegration of the entire Western Front developed rapidly'[1].

After the crossing of the Rhine and the subsequent encircling of the Ruhr, which followed immediately and was completed by the 1st April, the Allied forces in the North, rather than make for Berlin, were ordered to make a thrust for the Baltic; Berlin would have been more spectacular, but the drive to the Baltic offered the more solid advantages of cutting off all the German forces located in Norway, Denmark, North-West Germany and Holland[2].

The Battalion was given little rest after the consolidation of the bridgehead over the Rhine, for the Division, with armour in support, was ordered to move on a thrust line North-Eastwards, the 130th Brigade moving third[3]. The object was to make an all-out effort to link up with the Canadians, who had pushed well into North Holland, in order to cut off the Germans in the West and Centre of that country before they could pull out of the pocket that was being formed. The Battalion was to be completely mobile, every man and every thing being carried in vehicles; very little opposition was expected, and the daily distances were to be very long[4].

The Battalion left Anholt at 1330 hrs on the 1st April, crossed the frontier back into North-East Holland about a mile to the North of the town, and reached Varssefeld, about ten miles to the North, at 1600 hrs. By 0015 hrs on the 2nd it was at Geesteren,

[1]Eisenhower [2]Ibid [3]W.D. [4]Caines

eight miles on, and by 0700 hrs it had covered another twenty miles or so to reach Borsulo. The next serious obstacle was the Twente Canal, along which the enemy was entrenched, having blown the bridges, and the armoured advance guard of the Allies had already met heavy resistance there. A motor battalion was left to contain it, and the Guards Armoured Division drove East, outflanked the Canal, and captured Enschede at its Eastern extremity[5]. The 4th Dorsets crossed the canal on the afternoon of the 2nd, and at 1500 hrs reached a point three miles North of Gool, from where it was ordered to proceed with the capture of Borne, about nine miles North-East of its present position.

In the small hours of the 3rd the Battalion moved to its concentration area at Enschede, where it had breakfast, and at 1615 hrs, with D Company leading, it started on the road to Hengelo[6], which had been captured by the 7th Hampshires and 5th Dorsets[7], and thence to Borne. The bridge to the South of the village had been damaged but was still usable, and by 1830 hrs D Company had consolidated in the Southern outskirts. C Company passed through and secured the whole town against little opposition, and when, by 1915 hrs, B Company had passed through and mopped up the slight opposition along the railway to the West, the whole town was in the Battalion's hands. Only twelve prisoners were taken during the attack, but nineteen more were brought in by patrols and Dutch Resistance personnel during the 4th.

The Battalion spent five days in Borne. All the time it was there other units were continually passing through in relentless pursuit of the enemy[8], but for the local population these were five days of rejoicing. A procession, in which the C.O., the second-in-command and members of the Battalion took part, was organised on the afternoon of the 5th in honour of the liberation[9], the town square was renamed 'Dorset Square', and the C.O. and second-in-command were triumphantly pulled round the town in a cart drawn by some of the inhabitants[10].

On the 6th, the 43rd Division received orders to break out of

[5]Hartwell [6]W.D. [7]Hartwell [8]Ibid [9]W.D. [10]Caines

the bridgehead over the Dortmund-Ems Canal at Lingen on two routes leading towards Bremen. Early on the morning of the 9th the Battalion left Borne, recrossed the frontier into Germany, and soon after midday reached the area of Plenkorth, about four miles North-East of Lingen. But no break-out was necessary, for the one and only representative of the 'Wehrmacht' to be found in the whole of the neighbourhood was a deserter who was wandering round the Battalion area in civilian clothes.

On the 10th the Battalion was ordered to force the crossing of the River Süd Radde some four miles North-East of Haselünne, possibly capturing Herzlake on the way. It left Plenkorth in a North-Easterly direction at 1610 hrs on the 11th, and covered without opposition the dozen miles to Herzlake, which was immediately occupied, also without opposition. The Battalion was on the road again at 1430 hrs. The forced crossing of the river that had been planned proved to be unnecessary, and by 1830 hrs the Battalion arrived at Helmighausen, five miles to the North-East, still unopposed. However, the vanguard had encountered some slight resistance from small arms fire in the small town of Loningen, three miles further East, so the Battalion attacked. At 2020 hrs A Company moved off and occupied the East end of the town, but was held up by road blocks. Darkness hindered operations, and the position was not reported firm until 0130 hrs on the 12th.

The Brigade's final immediate objective was Cloppenburg, about fifteen miles North-East of Loningen[11], and late on the 12th the Battalion moved under cover of darkness to its assembly area two miles East of Lastrup[12], which the 5th Dorsets had been obliged to attack earlier in the day[13]. At 0115 hrs on the 13th A Company moved off and occupied Nicholt, about two miles ahead, where Lieut. Tom Wharton, commanding the Pioneer Platoon, was killed by a mine[14]. B Company passed through and occupied the cross-roads at Neue Kämpe half a mile further on. The advance was becoming increasingly difficult owing to the number of bridges blown by the enemy; the Sappers worked

[11]Hartwell [12]W.D. [13]Hartwell [14]Symonds

continuously bridging road craters and blowing up road blocks[15], and by 0600 hrs the whole of the Cloppenburg area was occupied.

On the 14th B Company was ordered to capture Bühren, a mile North-West of Cloppenburg, and to pass under command of the 7th Hampshires once the village was consolidated. It attacked at 1615 hrs, and by 1815 hrs reported that the village had been cleared; there had been no opposition, but twelve prisoners were taken.

On the 15th the Battalion moved some four miles to the North-West of Cloppenburg to occupy Varrelbusch, which had recently been taken by the Canadians. By the evening of the 17th the Battalion was established at Hagstedt, some ten miles to the South-East. Throughout these few days prisoners came in to surrender in groups of two and three, and on all its advances the Battalion met large numbers of Allied prisoners straggling back along the roads to the West[16].

On the 19th the Battalion moved to the area of Beppen, about fourteen miles South-East of Bremen. Several divisions were now closing in on this great port, and speculation was rife as to whether it would surrender or be defended street by street. The 3rd and 51st Divisions, South of the River Weser, were to make a feint attack on it, and then to try to enter Delmenhorst, using amphibious vehicles to cross the low-lying ground that was now flooded. The main attack on the city was to be made from the East by the 52nd Division, and the 43rd Division was to move round and protect its Northern flank[17].

By the 21st the 52nd Division had reached Achim, three miles South-East of Bremen[18], and it seemed clear that the main enemy strength had withdrawn into the city, or even farther North, and that only scattered and dispirited remnants remained outside[19].

On the afternoon of the 21st the Battalion relieved the 5th K.O.S.B. in Völkersen, about fifteen miles South-East of Bremen, where it had to put up with slight enemy shelling and mortaring during the night. It was now temporarily under command of the

[15]Hartwell [16]Ibid [17]Ibid [18]Caines [19]Hartwell

156th Brigade, which ordered B Company to occupy a small, square wood half way to Haberloh, about two miles further North, with a view to the eventual occupation of Haberloh and Hellwege, some three miles North again. A patrol left at 2200 hrs on the 22nd to investigate the road to Haberloh, and on returning at 0145 hrs on the 23rd reported the village clear of enemy. At 0230 hrs on the 23rd B Company set out for the wood, which occupied without opposition, and at 1830 hrs Haberloh was occupied by C Company.

The Battalion's next task was to occupy Hellwege. At 0230 hrs on the 24th C Company moved towards Stelle, about a mile to the West of the Haberloh-Hellwege road, and at 0420 hrs reported that the village, the hill and thirty-five prisoners had been taken without opposition. At 1030 hrs the rest of the Battalion, with A Company leading, started to attack a hamlet half a mile South of Hellwege, where it met determined opposition, but only for a short time. 'For awhile the battle was like hell let loose, as the enemy, with self-propelled guns, was holding out in the edge of a wood at the entrance to the village'[20], but at 1200 hrs A Company reported its objective captured, and D Company passed through and captured the centre of the village with very slight opposition, shortly after which the prisoners began to stream back; 129 were captured during the day. At 1400 hrs B Company began to move to the North-East of the village, and at 1600 hrs the Carrier Platoon relieved C Company at Stelle, so that C Company might attack the village from the West. By 1800 hrs it was entirely captured. The C.O. was wounded during the afternoon[21], and for the last hour or two of the battle the Battalion was commanded by Major Symonds. Later the second-in-command, Major M. R. Lonsdale, assumed command[22], and was promoted Lieut.-Colonel a few days later.

By the 25th, the 52nd Division was inside Bremen and was fighting in dockland[23]. The German troops were becoming completely disorganised, and the bulk of their forces was moving to the North of the town, but odd pockets of resistance were still

[20]Caines [21]W.D. [22]Caines [23]Ibid

holding out. On the same day the Battalion began to move Westwards towards Bremen, and at midday reached Bassen, six miles from the outer edge of the city; six hours later it was at Oyten, three miles closer in, and immediately moved off in the direction of Osterholz, with a view to capturing the Blockdiek area, in the outer suburbs. At 2000 hrs it was learnt that the 7th Hampshires had sent patrols into this area, where it had captured many prisoners but met no opposition, so the 4th Dorsets wheeled right at Osterholz and by 0140 hrs on the 26th had captured the village of Ellen, about half a mile to the North-West. Ninety-four prisoners were taken during the 25th, and a constant stream of prisoners and deserters was brought in during the morning of the 26th.

On the afternoon of the 26th the Battalion moved to Horner Vorst, still closer into Bremen, and on the 27th sent patrols out North to reconnoitre the River Wümn, which it was ordered to assault on the night of the 28th/29th, in order to form a bridgehead for the rest of the Brigade[24]; but by the 27th the 52nd Division was already in complete control of Bremen and the 7th Armoured Division was already driving towards Hamburg[25], so the operation proved unnecessary.

As soon as Bremen had fallen, the Corps was ordered to clear the peninsula between the Weser and the Elbe as far as Bremerhaven and Cuxhaven, at the mouth of those two rivers. Four divisions were to be employed, the 43rd and 51st Divisions leading[26]; the 130th Brigade was to lead the divisional advance on the axis Otterburg-Quelkhorn-Hepstedt[27], and the 5th Dorsets were to lead the Brigade[28].

The advance from the Rhine bridgehead to Bremen, where the Battalion saw its last serious fighting, had been to a large extent a rout; the remaining seven days of the war in Europe were to be little more than a prolonged mopping-up operation. The Battalion left Horner Vorst at 0700 hrs on the 29th, and spent most of the day leapfrogging from village to village on the main axis behind the 5th Dorsets. The 4th Dorsets met only very

[24]W.D. [25]Caines [26]Hartwell [27]W.D. [28]Caines

slight opposition, although the enemy shelled the road all day[29], and had advanced fifteen miles when it harboured for the night at Wilstedt.

The 5th Dorsets had encountered opposition at Tarmstedt, about two miles due North of Wilstedt, and had been obliged to capture it. On the 30th the 4th Dorsets were obliged to capture Hepstedt, about two miles North again[30]; the attack was to be in three phases, A Company leading[31], and at 0730 hrs the Battalion moved off. The advance was held up at 0800 hrs by mines on the road South of Tarmstedt; they were swept by the Pioneer Platoon under Sergt. Blandemer, who was awarded the Military Medal for his achievement[32], and A Company continued to advance, but was shelled while passing through the wood one mile South of its objective. By 1100 hrs A Company, with its supporting armour, was firm on the Southern edge of the village; at 1115 hrs B Company went through and secured the North-West; at 1230 hrs C Company captured the North-East; at 1530 hrs D Company secured the South-East, and the village was in the Battalion's hands. There was not much opposition, but shelling was severe, and a few casualties were suffered. The left flank was open, and the enemy was able to mortar the Battalion as it advanced along the road, which, in addition to being mined, was littered with blown up tanks and vehicles of all sorts[33].

During the afternoon of the 30th the 7th Hampshires passed through and occupied Breddorf, about two and a half miles further North[34], and on the 1st May the 5th Dorsets passed through and, with the 7th Hampshires, captured Rhade, about three miles on to the North-East[35].

At 0900 hrs on the 1st May the 4th Dorsets moved to Breddorf with orders to pass through the 5th and capture Glinstedt, three miles North-West of Rhade, and Karlshofen, two miles further on. The enemy was trying to hold up the advance by digging 500 and 1,000 lb. bombs into the side of the roads; they were fused by Teller mines, which exploded the bombs when vehicles passed

[29]Caines [30]W.D. [31]Caines [32]Citation [33]Caines [34]Ibid [35]Ibid

over them, an effective type of delay in a country that was so riddled with dykes and streams that détours were impossible[36]. By 1500 hrs a large crater in the road was bridged and it was possible for the Battalion to move into Rhade, where it was informed that the road to Glinstedt was impassable, and that twenty-four hours were necessary to bridge the road craters. It had no option but to return tamely to Hepstedt[37], where it found that all the accommodation was already occupied by L. of C. troops[38]. In fact the day was a ludicrous anti-climax in an advance that had generally been so easy that it was almost like a triumphal progress.

On the 2nd A and D Companies were ordered to capture the high ground East of Glinstedt[39], while the rest of the Battalion was to remain at Hepstedt[40]; at 2130 hrs D Company moved off, closely followed by A Company, and by 2300 hrs. patrols reported that there were no enemy on the forward slopes of the objective. At 2350 hrs the artillery put down on the objective and on the village itself a heavy concentration which lasted throughout the operation. A and D Companies' task was not difficult, as it was obvious that the Germans had withdrawn during the night, and the only opposition encountered came from a few fanatics[41]. At 0130 hrs on the 3rd A Company was firm on the South side of the little hill, and D Company was equally firm on the North side by 0230 hrs; at 0600 hrs the enemy opened fire on the newly gained positions, but at 1215 hrs B Company moved forward and occupied the high ground to the North without opposition; at 1300 hrs A Company occupied Glinstedt itself. During the afternoon the 7th Hampshires passed through and occupied Karlshofen[42].

On the morning of the 3rd the Battalion was ordered to drive North of Glinstedt and to reach the banks of the Hamme-Oste Canal[43], an order that was a great disappointment to all, as everyone was dog-tired and wet to the skin[44]. The canal was to be approached through Augustendorf. This village, which is about

[36]Caines [37]W.D. [38]Caines [39]W.D. [40]Caines [41]Ibid [42]Ibid [43]W.D. [44]Caines

twenty-five miles North-East of the centre of Bremen as the crow flies, consists of one straight street, on each side of which are houses standing back from it in their own gardens. It runs South-East—North-West, is over three miles long, and approaches the canal at right angles.

The attack, the Battalion's last action of the whole war, was opened at 1400 hrs by C Company, which occupied a wood one or two miles to the North of Glinstedt, and then patrolled forward to the South-Eastern end of Augustendorf. At 1515 hrs D Company moved forward to the left of C, and began to move up the village street, meeting no opposition but one Spandau, which withdrew when it was fired on. B Company followed C into the village at 2030 hrs and A Company began to move in at 2200 hrs By 2230 hrs most of the Battalion's transport was bogged owing to the terrible state of the road[45], which in places was knee deep in mud. A recovery vehicle managed to pull most of them out on the 4th[46].

During the 3rd May the Battalion made its way through the thickly wooded country and along the muddy roads to the outskirts of the village, meeting only slight opposition[47]. During the night of the 3rd/4th patrols were sent to the bridge over the canal at the North-Western end of the village, but returned without any information about the enemy; by 0100 hrs on the 4th all the Companies were firm in their positions, and there was no further movement on that day.

Early in the evening the information was received that the German forces in Italy had surrendered to Field-Marshal Alexander[48], and at 2115 hrs Brigade telephoned to say that the German Generals on the 21st Army Group front had met Field-Marshal Montgomery on Lüneburg Heath, and had accepted unconditional surrender[49]. The cease-fire order was received at 0800 hrs on the 5th May[50]. 'I cannot possibly express in words the joy that met our hearts on hearing the great news. It did not seem possible that the war for us had ended, after the eleven months of hell and horror that we veterans had endured from the

[45]W.D. [46]Caines [47]Ibid [48]Ibid [49]W.D. [50]Caines

beaches of Normandy to Germany. I could only thank God that I had been spared to hear this longed-for announcement. I never thought, as I explained at the beginning of these brief notes, that I would ever survive to hear and see the end of one of the greatest campaigns in the history of human warfare'[51].

[51]Caines

VIII

ARMY OF OCCUPATION

On the 7th the 130th Brigade was placed under command of the 51st Division and moved to the area of Beverstedt to assist in accepting the surrender and in the disarming of a German corps on the River Ems, and on the 8th moved to the area of Bremerhaven, where, on the 11th, the C.O. and 250 men took part in the victory parade at which General Horrocks, the Corps Commander, took the salute. On the 13th the whole Battalion attended a thanksgiving service held by the Padre.

The rest of the month of May was spent in the general work of collecting stragglers, displaced persons and suspicious characters, and in guarding key factories and dumps, work which involved one or two moves. When this was done, the Battalion's work as a fighting force was finished, and on the 30th May it settled down at Oerrel, near Soltau, forty miles South of Hamburg, as a unit of the Army of Occupation.

On the 21st November, the Battalion left Germany for Italy, where it remained until it was disbanded and returned to England. Major Matthews has written the following account of these months:

'The move from Oerrel to Bari in South Italy was made by train, through Germany, Holland and Belgium to Calais, then through France and Switzerland, and into Italy by the Simplon Tunnel. All appreciated the glorious scenery of Switzerland, and for a battalion too long accustomed to the sight of destruction in Germany, it was a delight to see a nation and countryside free from the scars of modern war. After a stay of two nights in the transit camp at Novara the journey was resumed, and Bari was reached on the morning of the 28th November, after a week's journey of 1,700 miles through six countries.

'At Bari the Battalion was under command of 54 Area, and for four months was engaged on garrison duties. Very little training was possible, but a number of cadres were run. The Battalion received a number of reinforcements, but lost many men on release.

'The Battalion's guard responsibilities included Area Headquarters, the hospital, a laundry, a Base Supply Depot containing 60,000 tons of stores, and the local jail, where the inmates included many dangerous prisoners of different nationalities. The use of two war dogs was a big deterrent to would-be thieves. There was a wave of crime at this time in Bari, and a number of operations were carried out to clean up the city. A curfew was enforced, and in conjunction with the Italian "Questoria" frequent patrols were carried out at night. During one of these night operations fifty Italians were arrested, and on more than one occasion shots were exchanged with thieves attempting raids on trains. Carriers were used on these night operations, which were planned with great detail and proved most effective in reducing the amount of crime, particularly theft.

'A number of ceremonial parades were held, and the Corps of Drums impressed the local population by "beating retreat" many times. On the 14th December the Battalion, in four companies, celebrated the King's birthday by a march past, at which the salute was taken by Brigadier G. P. Clarke, D.S.O. A salute of twenty-one guns was fired by the 4th Medium Regiment, R.A. A large crowd lined the route in mild weather and brilliant sunshine. The high standard of the troops on parade appeared to make a deep impression on the Italians.

'In January, 1946, a mobile column travelled 120 miles through the surrounding country, "showing the flag". The day was cold and—unusual in Southern Italy—a foot of snow covered the low hills a few miles inland from Bari.

'There were good facilities for sport, of which the Battalion made full use. The Battalion's football XI reached the semi-final of the Area competition and was fortunate in being able to use the city's fine stadium. Basket-ball proved very popular, and the Battalion won the Area inter-company competition. Hockey was also played, but the cast-iron grounds made playing conditions difficult for Rugby football. Nevertheless the Battalion's XV won all its matches and the championship of 54 Area. In the District final at Caserta it was defeated by the 2nd Field Regiment, R.A., by eleven points to three. The sequel was an invitation to play the City of Rome, an offer which unfortunately could not be accepted.

'On the 9th April the Battalion moved to Lazaretto, eleven miles South-West of Trieste, and less than a mile from the Morgan Line. It was now an operational unit once more, and with the 1st London Irish Rifles and the 1st London Scottish formed the 167th Brigade in the 56th (London) Division, which was under command of the 13th Corps.

'Lazaretto was an attractive spot, the barracks were good, and the Battalion had its own harbour and beach, with excellent bathing facilities. S Company was reformed shortly after the Battalion's arrival. For the first time since the 1914-1918 war it was in drill uniform. One of the first things the Battalion did after its arrival was to put on a large Victory Anniversary Parade in Trieste. Numbers of men returned to civilian life on release, but the Battalion received reinforcements, a fair proportion of which were "Dorsets", and also many others from disbanded units.

'The main task of the Battalion was manning the Morgan Line, which marked the frontier between the British-American Zone and Jugo-Slavia, controlling movement across the border at the road blocks, and active patrolling in the hills. Certain posts at strategic points were continuously manned. This was, in fact, the Southern end of the Iron Curtain, which now stretched across Europe from the Baltic to the Adriatic. A Company was located at San Dorligo, a village in the hills, inhabited almost entirely by Jugo-Slavs.

'There were frequent riots in Trieste, and clashes between pro-Italian and pro-Jugo-Slav sympathisers. Anti-British strikes occurred in Trieste and in the ship-building yards at Muggia, a large village a few miles from Lazaretto. Foodstuffs, particularly U.N.N.R.A. flour, were being illegally brought across the border from Jugo-Slavia into Trieste to feed the strikers, and so enable the strikes to be prolonged. An operation was therefore planned to impound these foodstuffs, which met with considerable success. A Company, for instance, seized thirty-three smugglers and impounded forty-one sacks of flour.

'When the Foreign Ministers of the Great Powers met in Paris in June to decide the future of Trieste, it was considered highly probable that Jugo-Slavia might decide to march in and sieze the town, at that time one of the nerve-centres of Europe, thus presenting the Foreign Ministers with a "fait accompli". The Division therefore prepared for action, and the Battalion was deployed in the hills along the Morgan Line. Positions were occupied, trenches dug, and platoon localities wired. Active patrolling was carried out, tanks and guns were moved up, defensive fire tasks laid on, and endless "O" groups held. Very detailed plans were made to deal with any attack on Trieste and a thorough reconnaisaance of the ground was made. At this time an N.C.O. jeep patrol from D Company drove over the line by mistake and was detained by an armed escort of Jugo-Slavs. They were returned safely the following day, after having been escorted back over a circuitous route by the Jugo-Slavs through their own positions, and so enabled to see everything! This situation lasted nearly a month, and when the alarm was over the Battalion returned to its normal routine. On the whole all ranks enoyed their days in the hills under semi-war conditions.

'Apart from this month, the Battalion was able to get plenty of sport. It was an extremely hot Summer and swimming proved the most popular pastime. Swimming and athletic meetings were held, and the Battalion did well in Brigade and Divisional meetings. The Battalion easily won the Brigade Rifle Competition, and largely through the efforts of the Dorset members of the Brigade team, the inter-Brigade boxing cup was won. Much cricket was played on matting wickets, both in the stadium at

Trieste and on the Battalion's own pitch, which was on the almost only level piece of ground anywhere around. This ground was overlooked by a Jugo-Slav outpost in a ruined castle on the top of a nearby hill, and the Jugo-Slavs must have wondered what was going on. The Battalion XI did well and reached the third round of the Corps knock-out competition, when it was beaten by the 1st Scots Guards.

'After five months at Lazaretto, the Battalion was relieved, and on the 14th September moved to Mestre, on the mainland near Venice, where it occupied some Italian barracks, with D Company on detachment in an aluminium factory three miles away. For a time the Battalion remained under the operational command of the 167th Brigade, but in October Brigade Headquarters was disbanded, and the Battalion came under command of 86 Area, whose Headquarters was in Venice.

'The Winter was intensely cold, and even Venice had snow. The close proximity of Venice enabled all ranks to spend much of their leisure in exploring that lovely and unique city. Football and cricket were both played, and the Battalion Football XI did well in the C.M.F. tournament. Cricket could be played until the middle of October, and many keen inter-company games took place.

'The Battalion's task was to carry out guard duties at the numerous forts and installations in the Mestre area. There were so many guards to be found that twenty-four hours on guard, twenty-four hours off, and twenty-four hours on again was quite the usual routine, and scarcely any training was possible. The Battalion was also responsible for four guards in Venice itself; these included 86 Area Headquarters on the Grand Canal, and one on an island in the Lagoon, where the Guard Commander had to take his sentries out by motor-boat, as their posts were half-a-mile by water from the guard-room.

'The strength of the Battalion was reduced by releases, and in October S Company was disbanded, followed by C Company in November.

'On the 23rd December came the sad (but not unexpected)

news that the Battalion was to go into "suspended animation" on the 1st January, 1947. The arrangements for Christmas were nevertheless carried through, and everyone had an enjoyable if a sad one. The Battalion was relieved in the first week in January, and on the 6th Lieut.-General Sir John Harding visited it and spoke to all ranks. By the 7th, most of the men had dispersed to their new units, and by the 3rd February, 1947, the disbandment of the Battalion was completed.'

While the Battalion was still at Oerrel, the Battalion Pioneers, helped by ex-members of the 'Luftwaffe', built a church in the camp area. This church was named 'Dorset Church' by the C.O., and on Sunday, the 30th September, 1945, the Padre, the Rev. J. E. Roberts, held a memorial service in it for the officers and men of the Battalion who had given their lives in the cause of freedom between June, 1944, and May, 1945. The last C.O., Lieut.-Colonel W. Q. Roberts, D.S.O., came out from England to read the lesson, the present C.O., Lieut.-Colonel M. R. Lonsdale, D.S.O., unveiled the memorial, and the buglers sounded the Last Post and Reveille[1]. As far as the 4th Dorsets were concerned, this memorial service was the last act of the war.

---

[1] Caines.

43RD DIVISION INVESTITURE
SERGT. F. STRETCH, 4TH BATTALION THE DORSET REGIMENT AWARDED THE M.M. 24.5.45.

PTE. H. APPS, 4TH BATTALION THE DORSET REGIMENT AWARDED THE M.M.
24.5.45

HONOURS AND AWARDS

4th BATTALION THE DORSET REGIMENT 1944/45

Number	Rank	Name	Award
90922	T./Lt.-Col.	TILLY, G.	D.S.O.
56230	T./Lt.-Col.	ROBERTS, W. Q.	D.S.O. and Bar
78201	T./Major	SYMONDS, G.	M.C. and Bar
105574	A./Major	HALL, R. F.	M.C.
CDN./60	A./Captain ('Canloan')	ANDREWS, E. G.	M.C. Killed 8th Aug. 1944
278530	A./Captain	McDERMOTT, D. L.	M.C.
247784	W./Lieut.	TILLING, R.	M.C.
285422	T./Captain	COTTLE, A. W. J.	Croix de Guerre with Gilt Star
	Captain/Q.M.	TITTERINGTON	M.B.E.
5727020	Sergt.	COOPER, G. H.	Croix de Guerre with Bronze Star
5726203	Sergt.	HOPKINS, P. B. G.	M.M.
5735051	Sergt.	SMITH, A. C.	M.M.
5617955	L/Cpl.	VIGG, S.	M.M.
6146660	Pte.	HYANS, P.	M.M.
14706830	Pte.	DRIVER, L.	M.M.
4406109	Pte.	LAWSON, V.	M.M.
5726812	Sergt.	BLANDEMER, J. W.	M.M.

Number	Rank	Name	Award
6025436	L/Sergt.	CHURCHILL, R.	M.M.
5726930	Sergt.	STRETCH, F.	M.M.
4926171	Pte.	COX, P. C.	M.M.
5734953	Pte.	APPS, N.	M.M.
5735228	Pte.	HILL, M. F.	M.M.
6343339	Pte.	WYNNE, J.	M.M.
6023331	C.S.M.	HARRIS, E. J.	M.M.
5729138	Pte.	MASON, W. H.	Silver Star (U.S.A.)
14694874	Cpl.	HODGE, S.	M.M.

MENTIONED IN DESPATCHES

269406	T./Captain	COLEY, C. F.	
	W./Lieut.	THOMSON	
5719502	R.S.M.	DREW, F. G. (M.B.E.)	
5731740	Sergt.	COAKLEY, C.	
5953769	Sergt.	WEST, J. H.	
2028585	Sergt.	NEWMAN, W. C.	
14380007	L/Cpl.	GRIMES, J. M.	

COMMANDER-IN-CHIEF'S CERTIFICATES

101737	Rev.	LEANEY, A. R. C.	For Gallantry
5726529	W.S./W.O. II (C.S.M.)	ALLEN, L. A.	For Gallantry
5725917	Pte.	MATTHEWS, J. E.	For Gallantry
5725836	L/Cpl.	KINGSBURY, J. E.	For Good Service
5727734	L/Cpl.	THORNELL, R. P. F.	For Good Service
5729138	Pte.	MASON, W. H.	For Good Service

4TH DORSET CITATIONS

BAR TO D.S.O.
LIEUT.-COLONEL W. Q. ROBERTS, D.S.O.

On the 26th March, 1945, this officer's battalion together with the 7th Hampshires were ordered to capture MILLINGEN and the high ground to S.E.

Due to the ground and a water obstacle, the only possible way to approach the village entailed a wheel through 90 deg.

Lieut.-Colonel Roberts was given the task of capturing the front edge of MILLINGEN as a first step, so as to allow the two battalions to pass through and capture the whole objective.

Just before the attack was due to be launched, it was discovered that a unit which had attacked before had failed to clear the start line for this attack. Lieut.-Colonel Roberts at once went forward and under heavy shell fire made a personal recce. and adjusted his plans.

The position was strongly held and about 150 Paratroops and Panzer Grenadiers were captured. The two battalions were then able to pass through and complete the capture of the whole objective.

The success of the whole operation was due to this officer's coolness and judgement under fire and the example that he set to his company commanders enabled a most difficult operation to be carried through successfully with very few casualties.

M.C.
MAJOR G. SYMONDS

Major Symonds commanded one of the leading companies in the successful attack on Eterville on 10th July, 1944. By his personal example under shell fire, and in the face of the enemy he proved himself to be a real leader, and he continued to inspire and cheer his men even after he was badly wounded.

BAR TO M.C.

On the 15th February, 1945, the Battalion attacked the enemy on the high ground EAST of the FOREST of CLEVE.

After passing through our own F.D.L.s, the left hand company came under accurate Spandau fire in addition to intense mortar and shell fire. In subsequent operation, the Company Commander, Major G. Symonds, M.C., displayed superb gallantry throughout. He was everywhere about the battlefield inspiring his men by his own total disregard for personal safety. The opposition was such that it was not until the third attack that the Company took its objective, killing some fifteen to twenty Germans of Battle Group 'Hutze'. Major Symonds was finally badly burned about the hands and face when the tank from which he was directing operations against a further strong point was knocked out by a Panzerfaust. He did not return to Battalion H.Q. until the situation was in hand, though obviously in very great pain. This officer's conduct and personal bravery were superb throughout the whole action and it was entirely due to his unsparing effort that his Company gained its objective and destroyed the enemy.

M.B.E.

CAPTAIN (Q.M.) H. A. S. TITTERINGTON

Throughout the campaign in N.W. Europe this officer has been Battalion Quartermaster. His efficiency, courage and devotion to duty has been of the highest order during the whole period. He has frequently brought up stores and supplies under heavy shell fire and there have been very few days when he has not visited the Battalion in the line or upon its objective. In December, 1944, in DORSET wood, NORTH of GEILENKIRCHEN, he came up every day and assisted materially in overcoming the difficulties of supply in appalling weather conditions under constant shell and mortar fire. He was always cheerful, always put the welfare of the troops before his own comfort or rest and his unsparing efforts have contributed very largely to the high morale of the Battalion.

M.C.

CAPTAIN R. F. HALL

During the assault crossings of the NEDER RIJN on the night of 24th/25th September, 1944, Captain Hall was i/c of an assault boat with men of 'D' Company. He made three attempts to cross the river, on the first two occasions the boat was holed by mortar or small arms fire and on the third was caught by the tide and washed down stream.

Captain Hall kept his party together and worked continuously in recovering boats to make another attempt. The river and banks were under fire throughout.

On the following night he volunteered to cross the river and made his way alone through woods, which were held by the enemy, searching for parties of the Battalion to organise their withdrawal.

Throughout the whole of these two nights he showed an offensive spirit and disregard for his own safety, which were an inspiration to all.

M.M.

C.S.M. E. J. HARRIS, 6023331

C.S.M. Harris joined the Battalion in July, 1944, as a Platoon Sergeant and has acted in that capacity from then until the end of the war. He was evacuated wounded for about a fortnight only in July, 1944. He has frequently acted as Platoon Commander when officers have been lacking and always with distinction. His great personality and outstanding examples of conduct did much to keep his platoon going, particularly at the SEINE crossing, TILLEY, ARNHEM and 'DORSET WOOD', and on the CLEVE-GOCH escarpment. He has done many patrols, always successfully, and his company commander has personally seen him destroy several of the enemy after an attack against machine gun fire. C.S.M. Harris's platoon was always well disciplined and most highly administered, even at the most trying times, in spite of having had numerous changes of officers and many casualties. He kept up his great enthusiasm and energetic leadership right till the end and always had the confidence of every member of the company, even in its worst moments.

M.M.

SERGT. J. W. BLANDEMER, 5726862

This Sergeant has either commanded or been Platoon Sergeant of the Pioneer Platoon since the Battalion landed in Normandy in June, 1944. Throughout that period his zeal and efficiency have been an inspiration to all members of his platoon. Since the crossing of the RHINE his platoon has done excellent work in dealing with obstacles and mines.

On the 30th April, 1945, the Battalion was advancing from TARMSTEDT to HEPSTEDT. The armour going ahead encountered mines between the two towns. Sergt. Blandemer immediately set to work to sweep and clear a path ahead of the armour undeterred by the shelling which caused casualties around him. Sergt. Blandamer's personal steadiness encouraged his men, and he and his men were specially commended by the Squadron Commander for their courage under fire in clearing the mines, and so allowing the tanks to go through.

The above action is but typical of many actions performed by this Sergeant in France, Holland, and Germany, and his cheerfulness and devotion to duty in the midst of danger cannot be too highly stressed.

M.M.

CPL. R. W. CHURCHILL, 6025436

On the 3rd May, 1945, 'A' Company had first captured the Ring Contour and the village of GLINSTEDT to its immediate West, against two companies of 15th Panzer Grenadier Division who withdrew in a westerly direction through KARLSHOFEN. Immediately after the capture of the village L/Sergt. Churchill was ordered to take a small recce. patrol to have a look at KARLSHOFEN and see if it was occupied, also to escort a Sapper Sergeant, who wished the check the road to KARLSHOFEN. L/Sergt. Churchill took his four men and the Sapper to the very edge of KARLSHOFEN where he saw some of the enemy behind a felled tree on the outskirts of the village. L/Sergt. Churchill was about thirty yards only from the nearest Germans. He was then fired on by two Spandaus on his right flank and some riflemen who were almost to his rear. L/Sergt. Churchill's patrol was to all intents now cut off. However, he got his L.M.G. and rifles into action and engaged the two Spandaus and the riflemen so strongly that he was able to keep them down and withdraw his patrol, and the Sapper Sergeant with them, unharmed, along a ditch towards GLINSTEDT.

He came back with exact locations of two German sections on the outskirts of the village and of the road block at the entrance to the village, also with the knowledge that the road to KARLSHOFEN was clear. All this was done with the knowledge that the Germans were almost certainly in the village and all the information, which proved to be accurate, was brought back within two hours of the capture of GLINSTEDT. There is no doubt that L/Sergt. Churchill's determination and bravery saved his patrol from being taken prisoner or destroyed by the Germans who were undoubtedly trying to get him in a trap.

L/Sergt. Churchill acted with great determination and set a high example of personal bravery, and all who were with him are agreed that it was due to his leadership that the patrol ever returned.

M.M.

CPL. A. C. SMITH, 5735051

On the 25th September, 1944, during the assault crossing of the NEDER RIJN Cpl. Smith and five men of his section were left behind as his boat was overloaded.

He immediately searched and found another boat and took his men across. After several encounters with the enemy, being unable to find the rest of his company, he took up a defensive position at dawn which he held till the following night when he received orders to withdraw.

He again searched and found an abandoned boat in which he brought his party back. Two nights later he volunteered to cross the river in company with an officer to search for stragglers.

Throughout the entire operation Cpl. Smith showed exceptional coolness and powers of leadership.

M.M.

PTE. L. DRIVER, 14706830

On 25th September, 1944, during the assault on the NEDER RIJN, Pte. Driver's Company Commander was seriously wounded in the legs after landing on the enemy shore. Pte. Driver, who was the Company Commander's batman, carried the officer to the river, found an assault boat and assisted him back across the river and as far as the R.A.P. This was done over 600 yards of river and ground, which was under continual mortar and small arms fire. By his initiative and courage he undoubtedly saved the officer's life.

M.M.

PTE. P. A. HYANS, 6446660

On the night 17th/18th October, 1944, Pte. Hyans was a member of a fighting patrol which was operating forward of the Battalion positions. While searching some houses the patrol was fired on from the rear and both Patrol Commander and 2 i/c were wounded. Pte. Hyans immediately took charge, personally killing at least three Germans, and by his initiative and coolness the patrol was able to return to our own lines with only one man missing. His leadership and personal bravery were an inspiration to the others. The action took place in the area DE KLOLS 763527.

M.M.

PTE. S. J. VIGG, 5617955

On the morning of 27th October, 1944, L/Cpl. Vigg was placed by his Platoon Commander in a position of observation about 100 yards in front of the platoon area. He remained there observing for some time, and heard the noise of wood being sawn. From his post he could not locate the exact position, so using his own initiative, he crawled forward a further 50 yards. He then saw four Germans sawing wood about 75 yards in front of him and various pieces of equipment lying beside slit trenches. He fired five shots killing two Germans and wounding the other 2. The noise of the firing aroused about 20 other Germans from the slit trenches, who opened fire and threw grenades at him. He withdrew back to his Platoon under heavy enemy fire. By his skill, courage and personal initiative he performed valuable work, obtaining information and harassing the enemy at close range. This action had a great effect on the morale of his platoon.

M.M.

PTE. V. S. LAWSON, 14406109

On the 20th November, 1944, the Battalion moved into a position N.W. of GEILENKIRCHEN known as 'DORSET WOOD'. The Signal Platoon laid line to all companies. Throughout the week the whole area was subjected to very heavy shell and mortar fire indeed. The line parties went out time and time again and communication was maintained under the greatest difficulties. Pte. Lawson of the Signal Platoon was a regular member of the line party. On the night of the 23rd November he went out three times to repair the line to the right forward company. Fire was very heavy at this time, but on each occasion Pte. Lawson was successful. Having returned to Battalion H.Q. wet to the skin, he volunteered to go a fourth time. Whilst in this sector Pte. Lawson's courage and devotion to duty were of the highest order. This example was a great inspiration to the rest of his platoon, who carried out their duties most efficiently during this period.

M.M.

SERGT. P. B. G. HOPKINS, 5726203

On 28th November, 1944, during heavy shelling in 'DORSET WOOD', N.W. of GEILENKIRCHEN, an ammunition pit containing

H.E. and phosphorous bombs was hit, causing the latter to ignite. Sergt. Hopkins, ignoring the imminent danger of the H.E. bombs exploding, without hesitation, jumped into the pit, among the ammunition, removed the burning phosphorous bombs and buried them. Had the H.E. bombs exploded, many men in the vicinity must have been killed or wounded, also the burning phosphorous bombs would have soon given away his platoon position and brought down still heavier enemy fire. By his courage, prompt resourcefulness and utter disregard for his personal safety, Sergt. Hopkins undoubtedly saved many of his men from death or wounds and set an outstanding example to his platoon.

M.M.
PTE. H. APPS, 5734953

During the Battalion attack on the high ground EAST of the FOREST of CLEVE on 15th February, 1945, Pte. Apps was a stretcher bearer attached to 'C' Company on the right.

Early in the action two of the four bearers were wounded and Apps was separated from the other bearer, who was working with another platoon. The company was under continuous small arms fire, mortar and shell fire, but Apps went out to attend the wounded time and time again, carrying several back to shelter of a building single handed until he was himself wounded by shell fire and had to be evacuated himself. His superb gallantry and devotion to duty throughout the action were magnificent and an inspiration to all who saw him.

M.M.
SERGT. F. STRETCH, 5726930

On the 26th March, 1945, during the attack on MILLINGEN, L/Sergt. Stretch was a section commander in the forward platoon of 'D' Company, engaged in house clearing. It was dark when L/Sergt. Stretch led his section into a large house. As one man went forward to cover the entrance hall, a German concealed in an alcove at the top of the cellar stairs, allowed the first man to pass and then leapt out, attempting to bayonet L/Sergt. Stretch, who immediately shot him dead. Realising that there were probably more enemy in the house, L/Sergt. Stretch immediately rushed down the cellar stairs alone, shooting at and wounding two enemy who were guarding the entrance. Firing his sten gun into the cellar he called upon the others to surrender, whereupon 27 Germans came out with their hands up, although fully armed with 2 Spandaus and two Scheisers and over 20 rifles. Thus this N.C.O., by his initiative, bold action and complete disregard for danger single handed killed one German, wounded two and took a further 27 German prisoners.

M.M.

PTE. H. T. HILL, 5735228

During the operation on the RHINE bridgehead, Pte. Hill was a bren gunner in No. 1 Platoon of 'A' Company. In the capture of MILLINGEN on 26th March, 1945, Pte. Hill displayed the greatest personal bravery and energy in supporting his section in house clearing operations. He bounded forwarded from house to house, shooting his section in at very close range and with the result a large number of prisoners were taken and few casualties were suffered in the section. On the 28th March, 1945, Pte. Hill's section was leading the attack on LANDFORT. The section advanced against considerable S.A. fire and reached the edge of the wood to the SOUTH of the house. Pte. Hill got up and with the greatest determination and bravery covered the section forward, firing his bren from the hip until he was finally wounded. His energy and personal example throughout the operation were an inspiration to his section.

M.M.

CPL. S. HODGE, 14694874

Cpl. Hodge joined the Battalion in July, 1944, as a private soldier. He was soon promoted and has commanded a section with great ability and outstanding bravery from then until the end of the war. He has fought at the approach to MT. PINÇON, R. SEINE, ARNHEM, HEINSBURG SALIENT, CLEVE FOREST and the RHINE crossing with great enthusiasm. At CLEVE FOREST he showed himself to be a very brave man attacking Spandaus with his L.M.G. by hip firing. He has taken part in upwards of ten patrols, as he was always a volunteer for this duty and on these patrols he has killed several of the enemy. Cpl. Hodge, who is only nineteen years old, is an enthusiast, with a bitter hatred of the Germans, which combined made him one of the most outstanding section commanders. For a short period he commanded the platoon with equal success. His efforts were second to none in his rank.

CROIX DE GUERRE
SERGT. C. H. COOPER, 5727020

This N.C.O. landed with the Battalion as a section commander. During the battles of ETERVILLE and MALTOT he was a leading section commander, and his initiative and leadership were an example to the rest of the company. He was subsequently promoted to Platoon Sergeant and during the advance through FRANCE was in command of his platoon on numerous occasions due to officer casualties. No matter what difficulties confronted him his cheerful gallantry had a great effect on his platoon, whose morale is always of a very high order.

M.C.
A./CAPTAIN E. G. ANDREWS (CANLOAN) (CDN/60)

During the battle for the village of ONDEFONTAINE on the 5th August, 1944, the above officer's company was completely cut off from the rest of the Battalion. Two self-propelled guns and approximately 100 infantry attacked his company, which at that time had been reduced to a total strength of 31.

For two hours Lieut. Andrews moved from post to post encouraging the remnants of his company, cheering and heartening the men.

It was entirely due to his example and leadership that all attacks were repelled and the position held until they were able to form up with the rest of the Battalion.

I consider that throughout the action this officer displayed exemplary courage and devotion to duty in the face of the enemy.

M.C.
A./CAPTAIN D. E. McDERMOTT, 278550

Lieut. McDermott after crossing the Neder Rijn on night of 24th/25th September, 1944, led his platoon up the hill to his company objective where a sharp engagement took place. The platoon suffered heavy casualties and Lieut. McDermott reorganized the remainder and took up a defensive position in a house, which he held until the following night, when he received an order to withdraw. As there was insufficient accommodation in the boat evacuating his party, he put his men in the boat and himself swam back across the river. On the night of the 27th he volunteered to cross again in a recce. boat and search the woods for any parties of the Regiment who might still be left and organize their evacuation. He penetrated the enemy lines and searched the objectives which had been given to the two left hand companies. He spent over an hour and a quarter searching the woods, which were now strongly held by the enemy.

D.S.O.

T./LIEUT.-COLONEL G. TILLEY, 90922

On the evening of the 3rd August, 1944, Lieut.-Colonel Tilley took over command of the 4th Battalion The Dorset Regiment and on the 4th August plans were made for the attack on ONDEFONTAINE by the 4th Dorsets. On the approach march to and crossing the start line the Battalion was subjected to intense enemy mortar and shell fire. A platoon of the leading company was wiped out and Lieut.-Colonel Tilley then extricated the company already committed and after examining all possible routes of advance himself prepared a fresh plan. All this time he was under the heaviest enemy fire. The enemy were later discovered to be withdrawing from ONDEFONTAINE and the Battalion was again told to occupy it. This operation entailed an advance through difficult country which still contained parties of the enemy. The leading companies, however, entered the village without difficulty, but were immediately counter attacked from two different directions and were in imminent danger of being destroyed piecemeal. Lieut.-Colonel Tilley personally ascertained the situation and with great difficulty extricated these companies and himself disposed them tactically just short of the village. Had it not been for his firm coolness considerable ground might have been lost. He was then able to bring very heavy artillery and mortar fire to bear on to the village, which caused great destruction to the enemy columns without incurring heavy casualties.

Throughout this action it was entirely due to Lieut.-Colonel Tilley's initiative and coolness in a critical situation that his Battalion was able to destroy large numbers of the enemy and complete its task with very little loss.

M.M.

PTE. P. C. COX, 492571, Att. 7th S. Staffs.

During the heavy fighting in the forming and holding of the bridgehead over the River Orne around M.R. 957534 west of GRIMBOSQ

No. 4926571 Pte. Cox, P. C., displayed the utmost gallantry and devotion to duty and complete disregard for his personal safety.

On the night 6th/7th August, 1944, Pte. Cox, a stretcher bearer, was attached 'C' Company for duty and in this capacity would normally remain at Company H.Q. until called for; however, he went forward to the leading platoon of his own free will under heavy small arms and mortar fire with complete disregard for his personal safety and attended to wounded in the open.

Shortly after first light on the morning of 7th August, 1944, the enemy put in a big counter attack. Pte. Cox organized the three other stretcher bearers with 'C' Company and led them to the forward platoons and supervised their work, which was entirely exposed to enemy mortar, artillery and small arms fire.

He organized the carrying of the wounded and accompanied them to the Collecting Point about 800 yards in the rear, the route frequently being submitted to heavy and accurate mortar fire. Later the stretcher bearers exhausted their shell dressings, and having obtained permission from the nearest officer, Pte. Cox returned to the R.A.P. about a mile in the rear, much of the route being subjected to mortar and artillery fire. Having obtained the necessary dressings and further stretcher bearers, he returned to the scene of the action immediately and continued his duties.

On the same day he returned twice more to the R.A.P., which had been moved, it being impossible to continue evacuation via the original route, and collected further stretcher bearers, dressings and stretchers and returned to his post, the route being subjected to shelling and mortaring. It was due to his initiative that the new route was found, and that it became possible to continue evacuation.

On 8th August, 1944, the Battalion position was repeatedly subjected to heavy mortar, artillery and Nebelwerfer fire. In spite of this on every occasion on which stretcher bearers were called for Pte. Cox responded immediately, leaving the comparative safety of his trench and attended to the wounded, in one case digging out a wounded man buried in a trench.

During the whole of this part of the operation wounded men could only be evacuated to the R.A.P. with great difficulty. Pte. Cox was very largely responsible for the organization and successful evacuation of the wounded and his actions were an inspiration both to the Medical Section and all who saw him.

CROIX DE GUERRE WITH VERMILION STAR
T./CAPTAIN A. W. J. COTTLE, 285422

This officer commanded 4 Platoon, 'B' Company, in operations until 10th July, 1944. At LE HAUT DU BOSQ (South of Cheux) he held the most forward position of the Battalion for four days and throughout this period displayed courage and powers of leadership well above the average. Subsequently he led a strong fighting patrol on Hill 112, which was ordered to destroy an enemy S.P. gun. The patrol was attacked by the Germans when it was behind their lines and thanks to Lieut. Cottle's energy and leadership a large number of the men were brought back intact from a very difficult position.

On the 10th July, 1944, he led his platoon into the attack on Etterville where he both gained and consolidated his objective under very heavy mortar fire.

He was shortly appointed Adjutant since when he has carried out his duties fearlessly and conscientiously in all subsequent operations in FRANCE and elsewhere.

SILVER STAR (U.S.A.)
PTE. W. H. MASON, 5729138

Pte. Mason was the company runner attached to Battalion H.Q. when the Battalion held Dorset Wood during the operation around GEILEN-KIRCHEN. From 20th-23rd November, 1944, his company held a very isolated position in the right forward corner of the wood. The company was frequently out of wireless communication with Battalion H.Q. owing to the distance and denseness of the wood. Responsibility for communication between Battalion H.Q. and the company therefore devolved upon Pte. Mason. Day and night he continuously made the 1,400 yards journey, carrying messages and acting as guide to patrols and ration parties. The route was subjected to almost continuous heavy mortar and shell fire, and there was no cover available. Yet Pte. Mason never failed to carry out any of his dangerous tasks, without any delay. Pte. Mason distinguished himself by his gallantry in action and by his devotion to duty under heavy fire ensured that communications with the company were maintained and that their rations were brought up.

M.C.
W./S. LIEUT. R. TILLING, 247784

On the 15th February, 1945, the Battalion attacked the enemy on the high ground East of the Forest of CLEVE. Within a few minutes of crossing the start line 'C' Company came under heavy small arms fire from automatic weapons from its objective and from unlocated positions on both flanks.

The Company Commander was wounded and the Company had suffered a number of casualties. Lieut. Tilling led his platoon forward to the cover of an old trench system and returned the enemy's fire. Then in full view of the enemy and under heavy small arms, shell and mortar fire he ran back to bring up the troops of tanks supporting the company. He rode on the leading tank and directed its fire against the buildings held by the enemy. He then rejoined his platoon and led them forward to clear the first block of buildings. Throughout the action his cheerfulness and disregard for his own personal safety were an inspiration to his own platoon and to the whole company.

M.M.
PTE. J. WYNNE, 6343339, Att. R.W.K.

For the past 16 months Pte. Wynne has been employed in various capacities on aerodromes. During this period he has frequently manned A.A., L.M.G., during air raids, and has on numerous occasions engaged enemy aircraft. On one particular occasion he was number 2 of an A.A. L.M.G. sited in a disused Bofors pit. An air raid developed and 15 Ju. 88s bombed the aerodrome, and a bomb landed on the side of the sangar knocking down Pte. Wynne and wounding him. He immediately picked himself up and got the gun into action in time to engage some ME 109s which were carrying out a low flying attack on the drome.

After the raid Pte. Wynne went to the A.D.S. for treatment, returning soon after and carrying on normal duty for the remainder of the day. Pte. Wynne's steadiness and devotion to duty under hazardous conditions, on one occasion although wounded, has been an excellent example to the remainder of the battalion.

www.ingramcontent.com/pod-product-compliance
Lightning Source LLC
Chambersburg PA
CBHW070204100426
42743CB00013B/3043